D0887335

INTO THE MOUTH OF THE CANNON

A Historical Biography of the 18th Arkansas Infantry
and the
Civil War in the Western Theater from 1861 to 1863

by

Robert Edward Reynolds

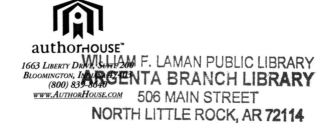

authorHOUSE™

1663 Liberty Drive, Suite 200
Bloomington, Indiana 47403
(800) 839-8640
www.AuthorHouse.com

First published by AuthorHouse 7/16/2006

ISBN: 1-4259-0605-2 (sc)

Library of Congress Control Number: 2005910732
Printed in the United States of America
Bloomington, Indiana

This book is printed on acid-free paper.

Into The Mouth of The Cannon

A Historical Biography of the 18th Arkansas Infantry
and the
Civil War in the Western Theater from 1861 to 1863

ACKNOWLEDGMENTS

I would like to thank all those who encouraged me to complete this work. Lois McGaughey was especially helpful by editing part of the manuscript and encouraging me to continue writing the book. I especially appreciate the assistance I received from Russell Baker of the Arkansas History Commission and all the staff there.

I would like to acknowledge Greg Potts, Park Manager, and the staff at the Port Hudson State Commemorative Area, State of Louisiana. Buddy Goodrum and I spent two days there walking the beautiful restored trails and earthen works, which gave us an idea of how difficult it must been for the Union army to mount an effective assault against the works. The many deep ravines that protected the Confederate breastworks were obstacles that would pose a challenge to any army attempting to take the fortifications. The time spent gave me a better understanding of why the siege was a real bloody affair. We were impressed by the amount of time the staff took off from their regular responsibilities and duties of management at the park to assist in providing information. Thanks also to Daniel Stoute for the spent time copying information that was helpful in my research.

During the course of my research I incurred many debts of gratitude. I would like to thank Robert Wood, Park Ranger at Fort Pillow State Park, State of Tennessee. The day spent there studying the restored Confederate works gave me a clearer picture of how hard it must have been for those laboring with pick and shovel to build such extensive line fortifications along the high bluffs overlooking the Mississippi River. I am grateful to the staff of the Memphis Public Library and the helpful assistance from Patricia M. LaPointe there, Special Collection Division; University of Arkansas Libraries, Fayetteville, Arkansas; Wesleyan University West Library, Fort Worth, Texas; State Archives of North Carolina, Office of Archives History, Raleigh; Wallace State College Library, Regional History Program, Hanceville, Alabama; The Corinth Civil War Interpretive Center, Siege and Battle of Corinth, Mississippi, and Fort Worth Public Library Genealogy, Local History and Archives.

I would like to mention Maxine Adams, for the contribution she made by sharing information on the Isaacs and Reynolds' family tree. I would also like to thank my brother Aubrey Reynolds who helped research the Isaacs family. We both have a common interest in Civil War History. His help and enthusiasm has been an inspiration to me.

To Charles Fontaine, a heartfelt thanks for the time he spent doing the final editing and the suggestions he made to improve the manuscript. Thanks to Deborah L. Reynolds for the contribution she made to the book by taking time out from her very busy schedule to help with some of the typing.

(All Civil War Clip Art courtesy of H-Bar Enterprises, Inc.)

TABLE OF CONTENTS

PROLOGUE

Many stories have been written about great Confederate icons, such as the Wizard of the Saddle, Nathan Bedford Forest, whose exploits have captivated the imaginations of many readers. This story is about a family in Saline County, Arkansas, and the hardships they endured during the Civil War. Four members of this family joined the 18th Arkansas Infantry: two sons served as lieutenants in the Confederate army, and two brothers-in-law served, one as a sergeant and the other as a private. The story follows Company H, Saline County Rangers and their trek from Fort Pillow, Tennessee, to the siege of Port Hudson, Louisiana.

The story centers around junior officers and the average Confederate non-com, whose face was browned by constant exposure to the elements, and often unshaven. His face was marked with sweat and dust. Dark stains of powder covered his face, which testified to the many battles in which he had fought. His hair was unkempt, matted with dirt and crowned by a weather-beaten old wool hat.

Crossing his back from his left shoulder hung his prize companion that he would not part with under any circumstances. The blanket role that dropped down to his right side contained one of his most prized possessions. Within its contents was an extra shirt. The bedroll on his back comforted him; he knew that in the warmth of this blanket, as he slept at night, he would have some protection from the unforgiving elements of rain and cold.

On his back was a greasy haversack, and attached to it was a flannel-covered canteen, which he borrowed from a dead Union soldier. He had learned that a dead Yankee could be one of his best friends, and to prove it he carried a United States Army Enfield rifle, which was supplied by the unresisting dead. His trousers were of different shades of blue and usually of the latest military issue, compliments of the Union army.

Johnny Reb was not concerned that his military dress was not the most up-to-date, but he was proud to know that he was distinguished from his enemy by a faded gray jacket that had been stained by the blood of his enemy … and his fallen comrades.

The women Johnny Reb left behind became equally resourceful as the war progressed. They had to improvise with whatever resources were available in order to keep the family alive. It was especially hard on Southern women who had to care for the young children and manage the farm. As the war progressed, shortages and hardships increased in the South, and it was not unusual for a family to go to bed hungry without anything to eat. There was no assurance that what little food that was stored away in some secret place would be safe from the age-old drama of hungry, foraging armies.

Many Southern men were idealistic and had romantic ideals about war. They were unprepared for the hard struggle that would lie before them. They were eager to whip the Yankees and felt they could quickly do so. They were especially eager to prove their fighting ability and to return home to the communities they loved as heroic children of the South. Those with wives and children had second thoughts, for their loyalties were torn between Southern independence and the responsibilities of fatherhood and farming, as well as other enterprises necessary to make a living.

The 18th Arkansas Infantry marched off into the mouth of the cannon, and at Fort Pillow, Tennessee, they got their first taste of modern warfare where their senses would become conditioned to the scream of shells passing overhead, seeking their next fatality. During the siege of Corinth, the 18th was called on to reinforce a Missouri brigade, only to find that the Missourians had retreated from hard fought ground they were trying to hold. Shouting "Butler" in one accord, the regiment entered the field and again faced the mouth of the cannon, for Battery Powell was bristling with artillery and had been reinforced at that very moment by an entire division. After the assault on Battery Powell, the regiment would rightly be called by the name "The Bloody 18th Arkansas Infantry."

CHAPTER 1

Follow the Sun

On the third of April 1865 a tradition was about to come to an end. Word had gotten to the residents of the little community of Tuscaloosa, Alabama, that Croxton's Raiders, a Union brigade approaching the city, was close at hand. Most of the citizens had retired for the night or were preparing to retire. Those citizens who were assigned to watch the approaches to the city spotted the Union brigade around midnight. An alarm was sounded throughout city, "The Yanks are coming!" Unfortunately, it was too late, for the raiders were then crossing the bridge.

Captain Murfee, commander of the corps of cadets at the University of Alabama, had given the orders to sound the long roll. Soon the entire cadet corps was assembled and ready for action. Brigadier General John T. Croxton, commanding the raid, wrote, "I could hardly hope to run over this force and take Tuscaloosa with 1,500 men (400 of them the 4th Kentucky, I had yet to hear from) supported as he was by 400 militia and 350 cadets, who filled the trenches around the city." Croxton cautiously waited for reinforcements before attacking and devised a plan to overcome the defenders.[1,2]

Captain Murfee shouted "Double time" as the cadets hurried to the center of town. As they rushed, they could see flashes of fire coming from Spencer carbines; the Raiders were well armed.[3] Skirmish lines had formed on both sides, and heavy fire was coming in. Captain Murfee gave orders for the battalion to take up positions behind the skirmish lines. Mostly boys, these young cadets were now facing seasoned veterans hardened in battle. The cadets were armed with muzzle-loading Springfield rifles. The battalion, ordered to lie prone, returned fire. Soon the enemy retreated back across the bridge, suffering some losses.

Three of the cadets were wounded. Captain Murfee was becoming fully aware of the gravity of his situation. If he continued to permit these young boys to fight, they would soon be butchered, for the Union army was regrouping for a counterattack. He had to act quickly or face the fury of every mother in Alabama. He ordered the youth to return to the university in haste. They were instructed to gather their belongings, to take only what they could carry in their knapsacks.

Parts of the town began to burst into flames as they were leaving. Turning back to look one last time, the cadets saw a glow coming from the burning buildings. Above the crackle of fire they could hear the shouts and curses of the Union cavalry as they continued burning the town. Even though the cadets had proven themselves as men, they knew they could never return again. The burden they carried because of their reluctance to leave the fight was further intensified by the hard reality of what they saw. The next day the University of Alabama itself was not spared.[4]

At the time Tuscaloosa was sacked and destroyed, the Isaacs were living in the little community of Cherry Grove, Arkansas, which is present-day Crossroads. Little Rock was the state capital and under Federal occupation when this incident occurred in Alabama. Little Rock was located about 30 miles southwest of the Cherry Grove community. Telegraph lines were open to Memphis, Nashville, and Chattanooga, Tennessee, which were being used by the Federal army as supply bases. General Sherman was using these bases to reequip his troops as he wreaked havoc on the Deep South in his march from Atlanta, Georgia, eastward to the Atlantic Ocean, thus cutting the South in half. Telegraph lines were the main means of transmitting news by North and South during the war, and both sides made it a top priority to keep the lines of communication open.

The news of the burning of the college and town, which happened in 1865 near the close of the war, was among the many upsetting reports and disappointing news the Isaacs would hear about throughout the course of the war. They had close ties in Alabama, having first settled in Tuscaloosa about 1824. Silas and Sarah had established themselves in the area, living in the vicinity of the college for 16 years and no doubt had made many friends and acquaintances there. They put down their first roots in Alabama, and while living in the state, five of their children were born. The family pursued education and always settled near centers of learning. The Civil War generated one wave after the other of devastating news which would adversely affect and change their lives. The fiery flames that had engulfed the university would reoccur throughout the war and things would never be the same.

Silas Isaacs married Sarah in 1824 at Tuscaloosa, Alabama, and they always chose to settle near a center of education. The University of Alabama at Tuscaloosa was endowed by the United States Congress in 1819 and was established by the state constitution the same year. The university was well established at the time they married. Silas and Sarah believed in education; their oldest son, James L. Isaacs, was a physician, and their youngest son, George W. Isaacs, worked as a teacher. George was studying to become a lawyer while living in Saline County, Arkansas, when the war broke out in

2

1861.[5] Silas' youngest daughter, Rose Altha Isaacs, became a schoolteacher after the war. Margaret Isaacs, another daughter, married a doctor, William C. Gillespie.

Isaacs would later move the family to Holly Springs, Mississippi, and this is enumerated in the 1850 Census of Marshall County, Mississippi.[6] Holly Springs was the county seat and by then had established itself as a center of culture and learning, having at that time four colleges. They were also attracted to Holly Springs because it had a Wesleyan community of believers to worship and fellowship with. The family must have received their education at one or more of the universities that they lived near on their trek to Arkansas. I have not unearthed any certificates of graduation for the Isaacs, but I can safely say, "They were educated somewhere along their journey west."

The Isaacs family and other early settlers moved west, attracted to the frontier by the prospects of productive land that was waiting to produce a bountiful harvest. The optimism that they shared with one another produced an intoxicating stimulant that compelled pioneers to move. Pointing to the fulfillment of their dreams, the early morning sunrise would beckon them to follow it to a hope and new destiny beyond the western horizon. Their enthusiasm was born of faith, knowing they were participants in a new beginning. Freshness lay ahead where they could build communities that would educate their children and where they would have the freedom to give thanks and worship God in churches that were just waiting to be built. Enterprisers would dream of gristmills to be built on waterways that would grind the grains produced from fields ripe for the harvest. Blacksmiths would hope for the opportunity to fire their forges and to beat and shape new farm implements that would be needed to bring in the overflowing harvests.

As the Isaacs and other pioneers pushed westward, their progress was not made without paying a price. The settlers were seeking a new life, and the Native American Indian peoples they were displacing were desperately struggling to preserve their way of life and culture that they had maintained for centuries. The Isaacs family left Pickens County, Alabama, and reappeared in the 1841 Mississippi State Census of Itawamba County, stopping there on their westward trek to a promised tomorrow. Itawamba County is located in northeastern Mississippi, and before white settlers entered the area it was part of the Chickasaw Nation that encompassed northern Mississippi.

Encroachment against the Chickasaw Nation by white settlers began in earnest in 1810. A staggering number of white squatters began to flow into the Chickasaw Nation in northern Mississippi, taking possession of lands that were ceded to the Indians by treaty, signed by the Federal government. For the next 20 years this intrusion continued unabated, creating continuous problems for the Indians and threatening their actual existence. Only token steps were taken to protect and ensure the future existence of these native peoples. The pressures of this intrusion into their territory became so bad that they were compelled to sign a treaty in 1830, but the United States Senate never ratified the treaty. The treaty only further served as a tool for the white settlers to press farther into Chickasaw lands in northern Mississippi.

The final solution to the Indian problem climaxed in the signing of the Treaty of Pontotoc on October 20, 1832. The Indians met and reluctantly signed the treaty at Chickasaw Council House on Pontotoc Creek. The treaty called for the survey of all Indian lands and the final removal of the Indians from their native Mississippi to the Indian Territories in Oklahoma. The preamble of the treaty showed the settlements were Chickasaw's. "The Chickasaw Nation find themselves oppressed and in their present situation by being made subject to the laws of the state in which they reside. Being ignorant of the language to the laws of the white man, they cannot understand or obey them. Rather than submit to this great evil, they prefer to seek a home in the West where they may live and be governed by their own laws."[7]

George W. Isaacs was born in 1839 in Pickens County, Alabama, and his sister Rose Altha was born in Mississippi in 1841, according to the census record. Some time between the two dates the family must have moved. This was after the removal of the Indian peoples in 1836 to the Indian Territories of Oklahoma.

The historical record the Isaacs left behind is a testimony to a life devoted to God. It demonstrates that they practiced their beliefs, keeping their faith in Christ and not wavering in the storms of life. The Isaacs were members of the Methodist Episcopal Church South denomination. Early Methodist worship services on the frontier were full of praise and prayers offered up to God. The Methodists during this period could be loud, and hymns of praise were enthusiastically sung, expressing their love and adoration for Christ. It was easy for others in the community to know their services were in progress because the Methodists of this period were called "Shouting Methodists."

The pioneers moved west, establishing communities in the wilderness, which soon drew ministers of the gospel into the new lands with dreams of spreading the Word of God. These preachers became the circuit riders on the frontier, bringing in an ingathering of souls. Unrestricted by the eastern establishment, they would spawn a revival on the Kentucky frontier that would usher in the brush arbor meeting and would echo the praises of the Lord throughout the frontier.

Out of this revival, unique to the western frontier, the Shouting Methodists movement continued to blossom and grow. It has been reported that their services could be heard for up to a mile. I can well understand this because they didn't have the distractions of our modern life like noise created from a constant flow of traffic bumper to bumper on our modern freeways. We have grown accustomed to background noises that have dulled our senses. I have talked to old-timers who lived during the period when the first Model T Fords were mass-produced by Henry Ford's assembly lines. Mr. Crabtree, a neighbor of mine who grew up in this time, told me, "You could hear a car coming miles away before it got there, and the exhaust fumes would linger on for hours after it passed."

True to the mind of the Kentucky revival, many Methodist churches would appear throughout the wilderness and one was established in the Cherry Grove Community. The New Hope Methodist Church, propelled by the holiness movement, appeared in Saline County, Arkansas, some time around 1850-1851. The Isaacs' oldest daughter, Elizabeth Isaacs, is buried in the New Hope Cemetery. The family's oldest son, James L. Isaacs, was the first to move to Calvert Township. When he moved there, the New Hope Methodist Church was the only Methodist church in Calvert Township, and they always chose a community of Wesleyan believers to settle near.

In the book Our Timberland Home, by Elwin L. Goolsby, the Reverend Elijah L. Crowson, who preached in homes before the church was built, gives a colorful account of the first revival of the New Hope Methodist Church.

"My father, Seth Archly, and my maternal grandfather, Edward Calvert, settled on what is now the old Dr. Richard C. Rhodes' place in the fall of 1838. Calvert Township is named for Edward. In my early boyhood days, society in the neighborhood contained a considerable element that was rough and wicked. The doggery and the dance reigned. My parents hated these things.

"We had no Methodist preaching in the neighborhood except at long intervals till about the year 1851 or 1852. There was a Baptist church (Shiloh) within one mile of my father's house at which I attended a Union Sunday School for several years. I think it was in 1851 we heard that a boy preacher was at 'Possum Walk Church' about eight miles from our home. Father went over to hear him and invited him to the neighborhood. The boy's name was H. R. Withers. He made careful inquiry about the neighborhood and told my father that if he and his neighbors would build a house for a Methodist church, he would take us into the circuit and preach for us regularly. Father came home and reported to his neighbors. All were pleased. Before the month closed a split and hewn log house was up, floored, and sealed, and the old-fashioned board pulpit was ready for the preacher.

"Father went to Possum Walk and reported the house ready. Said the preacher, 'Tell your neighbors I will preach in the new house on Friday night before my next appointment at this place.' He came and preached at the appointed time. 'One month from tomorrow,' he said, 'I will begin a protracted meeting here if the Lord wills it.'

"The time came, and meeting was begun, with the services at 11 a.m., 3 p.m., and at night. The meeting continued for nine days. At the close there had been 39 conversions and 41 accessions to the church. This was the beginning of New Hope Church. I was one of the converts of the meeting and joined the church. Father and mother also joined."[8]

The earliest record that I have of James L. Isaacs' presence in Saline County, Arkansas, dates back to May 26, 1855. The document is part of the minutes of the Quitman Masonic Lodge, which was active in Saline County during this period.[9] The document names Isaacs as one of the presiding officers of the lodge. This rare manuscript is located in the Grant County Museum located in Sheridan, Arkansas. In 1855 the lodge was located in Saline County, but this part of the county would later become Grant County in 1868.

The Quitman manuscript gives us a reference from which we can determine when he moved to Saline County. Based on this record it would be safe to assume that he was already well established before 1855, because Isaacs was well known in the community and a respected leader. Russell Baker, with the Arkansas Historical Commission, wrote an article for the State Association of Missionary Baptist Churches of Arkansas, writing about the same subject matter that has been discussed pertaining to New Hope Methodist Church and Shiloh Missionary Baptist Church in early Saline County. In one of our conversations, Russell said, "The Masons played a major role in the development of early Saline County."

The 1860 Census of Arkansas lists the Silas Isaacs family living in Saline Township, which is located in Saline County. Sometime later, Silas and Sarah moved to Calvert Township, which is located in the southern part of Saline County. This move might have occurred in 1861. Isaacs purchased 160 acres of land in Calvert Township on July 7, 1861, and was living near Cherry Grove during the time of the Civil War. The 1870 Census of Calvert Township lists the family as living there near the present-day town of Crossroads. It was not uncommon for early settlers to move often. Isaacs' journey west began in North Carolina where he was born, traversed Alabama and Mississippi, and ended in Saline County, Arkansas.[10],[11]

CHAPTER 2

A Call to Arms

Sir Henry Morton Stanley, who was a young man living in Arkansas during the early organization of Confederate units, wrote about sentiments of the period in his autobiography. Most of the cotton-producing states having seceded, it was only a matter of time before Arkansas would succumb to the emotion generated by the cries for war. Stanley wrote that the young men joined hands and shouted, "Is there a man with soul so dead, Who never to himself hath said, 'This is my own, my native land.' 'An honorable death is better than a base life, ' etc., etc., In the strident tones of passion, they said they would welcome a bloody grave rather than survive to see the proud foe violating their altars and their hearths, and desecrating the sacred soil of the South with their unholy feet. But, inflamed as the men and youths were, the warlike fire that burned within their breasts was as nothing to the intense heat that glowed within the bosoms of the women. No suggestion of compromise was possible in their presence. If every man did not hasten to the battle, they vowed they would themselves rush out and meet the Yankee vandals. In a land where women are worshiped by the men, such language made them war-mad." The emotions of the time were addictive, and under this fervor Stanley joined the 6th Arkansas Infantry and was sworn in at Little Rock.[1]

The winds of war were strongly blowing across the low lands of Arkansas. These were the regions of the state where the planters resided and cotton reigned supreme. The winds were not so strong in favor of secession with the dwellers of the hill country of Arkansas, many of whom had migrated from the Appalachian chain, which runs north and south, stretching from Georgia to western Pennsylvania. The sentiments held by the peoples of the Ozarks were equally divided between those who wanted to remain loyal to the Federal government and many who had migrated from the states of North Carolina, South Carolina, and Tennessee and were sympathetic to the call for Southern independence.

The hill country of Arkansas prior to the state seceding from the Union in 1861 had become a battleground between Union and Southern sympathizers. The discord between slaveholders and abolitionists would lay down the ground rules for guerrilla warfare that would dominate the trans-Mississippi theater of war during the conflict in Arkansas and Missouri. One of the main unwritten laws of warfare in the area would become, "No one will remain neutral and survive." Harsh vendettas and blood feuds were common and were used to persuade the undecided to take a stand; neutrality encouraged reprisals against family, friends, and relatives.

In the low lands of the Mississippi Delta and the southern region of Arkansas a fervor for war was smoldering, manifesting itself in oratorical calls for independence, "Give me liberty or give me death." The call for Southern independence was nearly unanimous, and the sentiments were echoed by both young men and old. In this part of the land men still worshiped women, and many women would accept no suggestion of compromise, encouraging their men to believe that it was their sacred duty to quickly whip the Yankee invader who was desecrating the hallowed soil of the South. Even in this climate of war rhetoric, however, voices could be heard calling for moderation and the preservation of the Union. These sentiments came mostly from the merchants and those who were engaged in manufacturing goods within the communities of the state.

In the election for governor in August 1860 Henry Rector was elected by a narrow margin. With a total vote cast of 61,198, Rector received 31,948 and R. H. Johnson 29,250. The election mirrored the division in the state during the period before Arkansas elected to secede from the Union, following in the footsteps of her sister southern states.

Several actions would take place before Arkansas passed an ordinance to dissolve its ties with the Federal government. On February 8, 1861, Governor Rector seized the United States Military Arsenal at Little Rock along with all the arms, munitions and supplies. Several thousand Arkansas militiamen as well as other citizens from different parts of the state had assembled at Little Rock for the purpose of demanding the surrender of the Federal garrison of 75 men under the command of Captain James Totten of the Second Artillery, United States Army. Realizing the Arsenal could not be held against such a large number of determined rebels, Totten chose to negotiate with the state government in order to avoid unnecessary bloodshed and elected to evacuate the post at Little Rock.

After the seizure, the Arsenal would be used as a staging ground for newly organized Confederate regiments. It was ideally suited for a temporary camp by Confederate units which were mustered into service. It covered 20 acres and was shaded by many trees, which made it a perfect location for troops to train and drill before departing to battlefields in northwestern Arkansas, Missouri, and assignments east of the Mississippi River.

A second step would plunge Arkansas into war, and there would be no looking back. The state government was fearful that the Federal military post at Fort Smith would be reinforced by Union troops from Fort Gibson, Oklahoma, and made plans to capture it. Governor Rector ordered a force of volunteers to proceed to Fort Smith, seize the fort, and take control of all the military property by force if necessary. Knowing superior numbers would overwhelm them, the small Federal garrison abandoned the post on April 23, 1861. Finding the Federal property unattended, the state's militia gained a bloodless victory, which proved be short-lived. In any future dispute over ownership of real estate in Arkansas, the prize would go to the winner on the battlefield.

The formal break came when the state legislature met on May 6, 1861, to adopt an ordinance that would dissolve the union that existed between the State of Arkansas and other states united with her under the compact entitled "The Constitution of the United States of America."[2]

Taking the Arsenal and Fort Smith generated enthusiasm and jubilation by those in favor of succession, but these bloodless victories would be short-lived. The Confederacy on the western front would from the start experience a series of tragic defeats soon after General Beauregard fired on Fort Sumter in April 1861.

Dr. James L. Isaacs enlisted as a physician, and was the first of the Isaacs men who joined the Southern army in December 1861. Casualties were beginning to mount in western Tennessee along the outer perimeter that defended the vital waterways of the Tennessee, Cumberland, and upper Mississippi River. These arteries were essential in order for the Confederate government to survive. Doctors and surgeons would be the first needed to treat the wounded and sick that would continue to increase throughout the conflict.

Following in his oldest brother's footsteps, George W. Isaacs enlisted as a private in Company B, Arkansas First Mounted Rifles at Fort Smith, Arkansas, on June 9, 1861, serving until October 31, 1861. Captain J. S. Pearson enrolled him at Fort Smith, Arkansas. Isaacs would serve under Colonel T. P. Churchill, who commanded the First Regiment, Arkansas Mounted Rifles.[3] Churchill's regiment participated in the Battle of Oak Hills fought near Springfield, Missouri, which is also referred to as Wilson Creek by the Union army. The regiment was ordered to take a well-defended hill during the battle. Several assaults were thrown against equally determined defenders. Churchill's regiment took the hill, but it cost a heavy price. "An Iowa regiment of Union defenders hotly contested dispute over ownership with volleys, unceasing musketry and well-positioned cannon fire."[4] Isaacs was one of those who paid a heavy price, for he was wounded August 10,

1861, on one of the assaults against murderous fire in the form of grapeshot that left its mark on him.

It must have been hard on the Isaacs when they received word that their youngest son, George, was wounded during the charge, because it was serious enough to require hospitalization for two months. This type of bad news would continue in one wave after another throughout the war, trying the faith of the Isaacs family. Isaacs was hospitalized at Stony Point, Arkansas, and after he was well enough, he returned to Saline County. While there, he helped organize the Saline County Rangers, Company H, 18th Arkansas Infantry.[5]

George must have been a very persuasive and determined young man; perhaps that is why he chose to become a lawyer. He stood 6 ft. 3 in. tall, had a light complexion, blue eyes, and light hair. That was above the average height for a Confederate soldier, who stood 5 ft. 6 in.[6] I have been unable to determine where he studied law. Saint John's Men's School located in Little Rock could be a possibility, but I have not proven this. The Masonic Lodge established Saint John's for sons of Masons, and Silas's oldest son, James, was closely involved in this organization. Isaacs was determined to reenlist because even though not fully recovered from his wounds, he helped recruit his brothers-in-law Granville M. McGuire and Richard T. Stockton as well as other recruits who helped form Company H. McGuire and Stockton married Isaacs women who were daughters of Silas: McGuire married Naomi J. and Stockton married Martha L.[7,8]

It might be interesting to note that at the time McGuire was considering his decision to volunteer for service in the Confederate army he was 31 years old and had four children under the age of 10.[9] During this period, strict draft laws were enacted in Arkansas. A large percentage of the Arkansas troops were assigned to posts outside of the state, east of the Mississippi River, after the Battle of Pea Ridge fought in northwestern Arkansas. This could account for why he volunteered; Southern men considered it a disgrace to be drafted.

Stockton and McGuire enlisted and George Isaacs reenlisted at Little Rock, Arkansas, on March 3, 1862. Many Southern men were idealistic and had romantic ideals about war. They were unprepared for the hardships and suffering that would be required of them, but they were fully persuaded in the virtue of their cause and were willing to fight to secure Southern independence. Like a lot of young men of this period, they were eager to prove their manhood on the field of valor and felt they would quickly whip the Yankees and proudly return to those they loved and the community they respected. Little did they know they were about to embark on a crusade that would end in utter destruction and devastation of their beloved Southern homeland. Like a gentle breeze that nudged them on, inspiring them into battle, it would turn on them in a storm of agony and death that would fill the air with the roar of cannon, musketry, and the deadly scream of canister as it passed overhead on its way to kill and maim.

The 18th Arkansas numbered about 1,000 men strong and was first ordered to Corinth, Mississippi, but the order was countermanded at Memphis, according to R. T. Martin, a member of Company G, 18th Arkansas. Martin's company was transported on a small steamer to DeValls Bluff on the White River, arriving on March 9, 1862, and from there they traveled by rail to Argenta, which was across the river from Little Rock. While at Little Rock his company was sworn into service by Governor Rector, and after that they made the return trip by rail back to DeValls Bluff. He wrote an article about the 18th which appeared in the 1909 issue of The Confederate Veteran. Martin wrote, "We were sent to Island No. 10 on the Mississippi River. Before we reached that place the Federals had possession of it and we fell back to Fort Pillow. I remember seeing some of our unfortunate comrades floating down the river on logs, who were rescued by members of our company." They picked up some of the survivors of Island Number 10 who escaped capture.

Company H was also sworn in at Little Rock by Governor Rector and then was transported by train on the Memphis and Little Rock Railroad to DeValls Bluff where they were organized into a regiment. From there they moved by steamer down the White River to the mouth of the Mississippi, then continued upriver to their assignment. The regiment made a stop at Memphis, Tennessee, and then were transported by steamer from there to Fort Pillow after receiving their new orders.[10,11]

On April 3, 1862, a notice appeared in the Arkansas Gazette which notified the public about scheduled train departures from Little Rock to DeValls Bluff. Also in this schedule were timetables for the return trips back to Little Rock on the recently completed western stretch that ran from the Arkansas River to the White River, a distance of 49 miles which took three to four hours of travel time. Oftentimes, during the dry summer months, the Arkansas River become too shallow for steamships to navigate the river channel from Little Rock to DeValls Bluff. The completion of the railroad helped the Confederate military move large numbers of troops and equipment quickly in the early stages of the war in Arkansas. The western leg of The Memphis and Little Rock Railroad was completed on January 26, 1862. The Gazette notice, which appeared in early April, confirms Martin's story and the date his company made the trip by rail. During this period, DeValls Bluff was one of the main landings on the White River for steamboats traveling to the Mississippi River.[12,13]

Fort Pillow Bluffs and Batteries

Fort Pillow, Tennessee, was located on the Mississippi River 60 miles above Memphis. The site was ideally located because it was situated on high bluffs, overlooking the river. The Chickasaw Bluffs provided the Confederates with a strong point to defend against Federal gunboats attacking from the river.

Early in the war, in 1861, the Confederate army built extensive fortifications along these bluffs as part of a defensive network that protected the upper Mississippi Valley from a Union advance by water. The high bluffs were named after the Chickasaw Indians, who roamed the area before white settlers moved in.

The bluffs offered a panoramic view of traffic on the river as commerce traveled up and down the Mississippi. Several places were chosen along the bluffs that would provide the best possible place to build forts and defend the river. Fort Randolph, a smaller work above the town of Fulton was located south of the mouth of the Hatchie River. Fort Wright's exact location is unknown, and Fort Harris was built above Memphis and was designed to defend the city. Fort Pillow was the largest and was named after General Gideon Pillow, a veteran of the Mexican war.[14] Soon after they enlisted at Little Rock, the three men were assigned to this post in 1862. They were part of the river brigade that made up a defensive line of forts and fortifications on the Mississippi.

The muster rolls of the 18th list Granville sick and on leave from March 3, 1862, to March 3, 1863. A measles epidemic broke out soon after the

Arkansas 18th arrived at DeValls Bluff, Arkansas, on their way to Fort Pillow and could account for his absence during this period. The epidemic played havoc with the 18th, reducing their numbers and sending others home sick. Eventually he recovered and was well enough to return to duty at Port Hudson, Louisiana, in early 1863.[15]

While Lieutenant Isaacs and Sergeant Stockton were assigned to Fort Pillow, a series of naval engagements took place between Union gunboats and Confederate naval vessels call Rams. The Confederates were attempting to silence the heavy siege mortars the Union had employed to throw 13-inch bombs at the fortifications from a safe distance of two miles. Surprising, as it may seem, it wasn't the exploding shrapnel that threatened the fort, it was the health of the defenders. The regiment continued to be devastated by sickness and disease while stationed at Fort Pillow. This must have been a rude awakening to the reality of the Civil War and prophetic of things to come. Sickness and disease would become the two grim reapers that would harvest death throughout the war.

Second Lieutenant Benjamin F. Hancock, Company K, 18th Arkansas Infantry wrote the following letter while he was stationed at Fort Pillow during a repulse of Federal gunboats on April 15, 1862. The original letter contains a hand-drawn map showing the location of where the 18th Arkansas was camped on the day Hancock wrote the letter. The regiment was positioned on the extreme north end of the fort, and because of this they were exposed to the first incoming shells from the Union fleet moving down river. Benjamin writes about the uncertainty of death and feels disease is their greatest threat. The original hand-written letter is hard to read and some editing was necessary, but little was changed in order to preserve the writing style of the period.

Dear Mr. Wilson,

"Nothing but the circumstances would induce me to write you a letter tonight. For I have been suffering all day with sore throat, in-fact I took my "pallet" this morning and should have suffered all day if Lincoln's gunboats had not Hoisted me out. Our fleet way up the river and about 10:00 o-clock they came around the point in regular Gilpin style, and in a few minutes -- things was humpy and bristle around the batteries-getting the fleet into battle line and about 11:30 o-clock we could see the Lincolnites about 2 miles from us a-cropt the point, presently 3 of their boats came around the point in full view, when we were formed into lines and march off to the ordinance Dept for our boxes, ammunition and colors. Our batteries opened on them and find several guns, the balls falling all around their boats, which took the hint and "double quick" back behind the point without returning our fire, and then they had been lying low since keeping up steam and us in sunshine all the while. What they are doing is more than we know, but the general impression is that they are either landing troops this side to come down and attack us simultaneously with their gunboats, or that they are cutting a-crop the point to plant a battery below us and cut off communications between us and Memphis. Either suggestion is plausible and I feel satisfied that we will know what is up by morning. We had just heard orders to stick with our point and with our arms by our sides. It is strange but while we were, and expecting a fight any minute. I never felt more like having fun in my life. Notwithstanding I was sick enough to be in bed. I never was in a better humor and when I would try to think over it seriously and appreciate the danger. I would find myself laughing at some poor fellow who really appreciated his position. And our whole Company learned to share my feelings for every fellow was cutting at his neighbors while you could see men from other companies with long and serious faces perhaps thinking of home and the dear ones left behind, and it is really a serious thought, for we hear ahead something for a fight in a day or two, and in that fight some of us will have to "bite the dust." Who knows whom it will fall upon. We all share the same change and in-fact we had two changes certain against uncertainties. I mean bullets and disease, and I believed the latter is the more destructive of the two. And now I'm getting serious. I will give you an idea of the river at this point.

"You will see that our regiment is on the extreme right of the fort and now exposed to within their shelling, or their land forces than any other regiment. Colonel Carroll has been trying to have us moved but there is no good camping ground, and I suppose we will have to tough it out. I thought I could draw a better river, but I think another attempt will convince me that I am no artist, however this might give you some idea of how we stand at 10 o'clock tonight, and now hoping that the end of the war may smile upon the cause of the just."[16]

E. F. Sanders, a Confederate soldier who was stationed at Fort Pillow, wrote a letter on April 22, 1862, about the weather conditions at the post. Parts of his letter have been edited. The soldier writes about the drudgery of the war and the miserable conditions caused by the weather, which would continue to make life miserable in the camps in which the 18th would live in the future.

Dear Brother and Sister,

"I have not much to write you since I have been here just a week and it has been raining ever since. It has been raining ever since we left Little Rock. Oh we have had it bad. We had hurricane passage in the rain to this, they was just as thick as they could stand up down on cabin & first deck. We land in sight 5 in number & then for the first time I had the pleasure of looking at them. They are a dangerous looking trick. I don't like the looks of them a tall. They opened the ball & have been bombarding us ever since till yesterday they have been laying around behind a bank in the river throwing in our camps, but have not damaged us but very little. They killed one mule & crippled one man out of 275 shots & it is thought that we sunk one of their boats. But certain the river is up very high all over the bottoms everywhere & thing. The enemy cut a road through the bottom & made a raft to put 2 of their Guns to keep boats from coming from Memphis by the river. But our Gun Boats was watching their movements & taken both of the guns from them & they are planted here on the river now."[17]

The price of holding onto this strategic position by the Confederate defenders was apparently becoming too costly. General Sidney Johnson had retreated from Kentucky and had suffered a disastrous defeat at Shiloh. To compound the defeat Johnson was killed during the battle. The mangled Southern army commanded by General Beauregard limped its way back to fortified Corinth, Mississippi. Southern strategists knew they could no longer hold Corinth and anticipated an attack upon the fortifications. After Shiloh, the Union began concentrating its strength above Corinth. Expecting an advance by General Henry Halleck's Union army, the Southern army moved south of Corinth, forming a line of defense along the Mobile and Ohio Railroads. Fort Pillow was essentially cut off from the main body of Southern forces. On June 4, 1862, the Confederate command ordered the evacuation of the fort. During that night explosions and heavy clouds of smoke were seen billowing from the Fort. As a final salute to the besiegers a brilliant flash was observed illuminating the night as Confederates spiked the larger cannons and blew the casements, magazines, and breastworks in a final farewell at their departure.[18],[19]

Edwin Sessel witnessed the destruction of Fort Pillow and wrote a letter to his cousin, dated August 14, 1862, from Abbeville, Mississippi. He wrote, "That night the artillery regiment left, we commence the work of destroying our guns and property. First we set fire to the quartermaster stores, next, the commissary, and then every shanty on the hill. We blew up all the guns, except two, which would not burst. It was a terrific sight-the rain pouring down, the thunder rolling midst the lightning flashes, while the Yankees were pouring a stream of fire, making the sight sublime, though terrible."[20]

CHAPTER 3

The Civil War Surgeon

Typical Field Hospital

James Isaacs, like his younger brother George, helped recruit a company of volunteers early in the war. James settled in Saline County before his father. Later, Silas brought the rest of the family to Arkansas. Perhaps the younger George was following the example of leadership that the oldest brother demonstrated in his ability to persuade others to rally behind the Southern cause. James was a leading citizen of Saline County and a presiding officer in the Masonic Lodge. The Masons played a large role in the development of this part of the state and many held public office.

On arriving in the county, James began to purchase large tracts of land, hoping to speculate on the future expansion and growth of the area. His real estate holdings were numerous and extensive, covering thousands of acres of land. He continued to buy land up to the start of the war, but like a lot of dreams and hopes of early pioneers in Saline County, his enterprising energies would be derailed by the tragic events of the war.[1]

His influence and trust were sought out. This is evident in a letter sent from a Confederate soldier stationed at Port Hudson in 1863 to his family in Saline County. The soldier sent 40 dollars by Tom Page to be delivered to Isaacs and entrusted into his care. He was then to manage the money for the soldier's family as needed.[2]

Isaacs' official military record lists him on the register of commissioned officers of the Provisional Army of the Confederate States. He was stationed at Island No. 10 in December 1861. His record lists him as serving in the 11th Regular Arkansas Infantry Volunteers on February 17, 1862, at New Madrid, Missouri. He had been appointed surgeon on June 19, 1861, in the 11th Regular Arkansas Infantry Volunteers, Company I and was assigned to the river brigade at Fort Pillow, Tennessee, on October 25, 1862.[3],[4]

The following letter was written by Doctor Isaacs and is part of the historical basis for the research I did on the Civil War surgeon. Isaacs was a member of R. E. Lee Camp Number 158, United Confederate Veterans of Tarrant County, Fort Worth, Texas. He is listed as serving in the 11th Arkansas Infantry on roster of officers of Camp 158 after the war. He served as a staff surgeon and in Poke's Corps, Army of Tennessee, during his enlistment in the army. He helped recruit and organize Company I in Saline County, Arkansas. I found his camp records in the Fort Worth Public Library, and without the helpful assistance from the genealogy department I would not have obtained this document. The transcript is hand written by Isaacs and reveals much about his military record. Even though it is brief and does not go into detail, it contains many interesting stories that helped me retrace his military record.

"At an early day I assisted in organizing a company in my immediate vicinity, L. H. Moony, Captain, and was elected Second Lieutenant after the organization of the regiment 11th Arkansas Infantry. I was selected by Colonel J. M. Smith as his staff surgeon in which capacity I served till the capture of my Regiment at Island Number Ten and Madrid Bend. Being sick at the time and absent from my command, I escaped capture. So soon as I was able for duty, I reported and was given a position in the Overton Hospital, Memphis General, Dr. Mastin of Mobile, Alabama, post surgeon. After remaining there for a short time, I was ordered to report for duty at the headquarters of General Bragg's division of the Army of Corinth, Mississippi. Dr. A. J. Ford, surgeon medical director, was assigned to hospital duty on the Mobile and Ohio Railroad. I established and put in working order hospitals at Guntown, Tupelo, Mississippi, in which was subsequently the headquarters of the army. My regiment was on detached duty at Fort Pillow

Island Number Ten, united with the 12th Arkansas Infantry at New Madrid, Missouri. I was not engaged in any important battles during my connection with the Army, except as surgeon."[5]

Because of the fall of Fort Donaldson and Fort Henry, the outer perimeter of defenses that protected western and middle Tennessee left the city of Memphis, Tennessee, exposed to Union attack by river. Memphis was the first major river port located on the Mississippi River below Federally held territory. The city's strategic location would play a significant role for both North and South during the course of the war. Memphis had an existing hospital and hotels that would be used as facilities to treat the sick and wounded of both sides.

The community got its first realization how bloody the war was to become after the Battle of Belmont, Missouri, fought November 7, 1861. When the casualties began to arrive in Memphis, the Overton Hotel was converted into a military hospital to treat the wounded. Construction on the Overton Hotel had begun in 1858 and was near completion when it was seized in January 1862 by Confederate authorities to accommodate the mounting casualties that were pouring into Memphis.

From the start of hostilities in the Western and trans-Mississippi Theater, the citizens of Memphis responded to the crisis wholeheartedly by providing large quantities of bedding, linens, bandages, clothing, and food for the sick and wounded Southern soldiers. Prominent women of Memphis played major roles in setting up hospitals and caring for the sick in private homes. This began in June 1861 and the buildup of accommodations to provide medical care would continue up to the Battle of Shiloh fought near Pittsburgh Landing on the Tennessee River. By January 1862 there were 1,000 hospital beds in the city.

Soldiers who first contracted measles in camps teeming with disease would fill many of these beds. Measles would act as a catalyst, weakening the body's immune system, which would open the door to more crippling diseases. Upper respiratory infections, such as tuberculosis, pneumonia, and bronchitis, would continue to kill and disable those who first contracted measles. This could be why Doctor Isaacs had to resign his commission while stationed in Mississippi.

Measles was running rampant through the ranks of Arkansas troops stationed along the upper Mississippi Valley. Thirty-seven men of the 18th Arkansas and 27 men of Doctor Isaacs' 11th Arkansas are buried at Elmwood Cemetery located in Memphis, Tennessee. The names inscribed on the tombstones there are a mute testimony to epidemics and those who died from their wounds. There are approximately 984 Confederates buried at Elmwood that died between October 1861 and May 1862. Many of these soldiers died in hospitals in Memphis during this period. During the Civil War the Southern Army suffered a 20 percent casualty rate; Memphis hospitals must have cared for over 5,000 Confederates based these figures. Almost all of those who are buried at Elmwood were from Tennessee, Texas, Missouri, and Mississippi, with the largest percentage from Arkansas.[6]

Patricia M. LaPointe wrote about this subject in the Tennessee Historical Quarterly: "Crowded together in the army camps, raw recruits, many of whom had never been exposed to infantile diseases and had never been vaccinated, were ready targets for the mumps and smallpox that followed epidemic attacks of measles. Outbreaks of typhoid fever and the ailment commonly called "diarrhea-dysentery" were the result of poor sanitation and contaminated water. Exposure and lack of proper clothing resulted in colds, pneumonia, and other respiratory infections. Summer brought epidemic outbreaks of malaria, especially among the soldiers fighting in the Mississippi Valley, Confederate troops, to a much greater extent than Union troops, also suffered from scurvy, a dietary deficiency disease."[7]

The Confederacy on the western front had experienced a series of tragic defeats soon after General Beauregard opened fire on Fort Sumter in April 1861. The first lines of defense that protected the vital waterways that were essential to the survival of the Western and trans-Mississippi Confederacy began to fall under an aggressive campaign by Northern strategists. It was realized early in the war that in order to defeat the South her railroads and waterways would have to be securely in Union hands.

The Confederacy had constructed defenses to protect the northern-most approaches to the Mississippi, Tennessee, and Cumberland River. Fort Donaldson on the Cumberland and Fort Henry on the Tennessee were strategically located near the Kentucky border. Island Number 10 near New Madrid, Missouri, Fort Pillow, and Fort Randolph, all located north of Memphis on the Mississippi River served as a barrier to prevent a Northern invasion of the Upper Mississippi Valley.

Island Number 10 was located above New Madrid Bend, situated in the middle of the river, and was chosen because it could be easily fortified. Confederate strategists planned to heavily fortify the Island, hoping this fortress in the river would stop the Union from encroaching on Southern-held territory below New Madrid, Missouri. During July of 1861, General Gideon Pillow ordered the construction of fortifications on the Island. His plans would never be fully implemented until General Polk took command of the district. After General Polk moved his headquarters to Columbus, Kentucky, work was resumed on the defenses, and the Island was heavily fortified under his direction. Isaacs was assigned to this post in December 1861 and served as a staff surgeon with the 11th Arkansas Infantry. Island

Number 10 was garrisoned by about 7,000 troops when it surrendered to General John Pope on April 7, 1862. During this period, Isaacs was on leave because of sickness and was not taken prisoner after the surrender.[8]

Isaacs soon recovered from his illness and was assigned to the Overton Military Hospital as a staff surgeon under the direction of Dr. C. H. Mastin, chief supervisor of all hospitals in Memphis. Large numbers of wounded and sick Confederate soldiers were arriving in Memphis by steamer, and local civic leaders of the city helped to complete the transition of the Overton Hotel to a military hospital. The hospital was equipped with an operating room, pharmacy, and offices to accommodate the surgeons on staff. Isaacs along with others in the medical field would be hard pressed to treat a flood of casualties from the retreating Southern armies that would pour into Memphis.

During the winter of February 1862 the Union army based at St. Louis captured Fort Henry and Fort Donaldson. The Union victories forced General Albert Sydney Johnson to withdraw from southern Kentucky and much of western and middle Tennessee, leaving the area open to Union occupation. General Johnson withdrew farther south to Corinth, Mississippi, and established a strong defensive line covering the Memphis and Charleston Railroad. The success of the Union advances south was applying pressure on General Johnson to put a halt to any further advances into Southern territory. Under the leadership of Johnson a Confederate buildup of arms and supplies was being concentrated at Corinth. This was made possible by the strategic location of Corinth, which served as a railroad center.

In late March 1862 Johnson felt confident that the Confederate army was in sufficient strength to make a push north and drive the Yankee invader out of Tennessee. Johnson knew the time was running out because General D. C. Buell's Army of Ohio was moving from Nashville and soon would join General Grant. On the morning of April 6, 1862, Johnson told his fellow officers, "Tonight we will water our horses in the Tennessee." Johnson's huge, powerful Army of Mississippi, composed mostly of unseasoned units, would soon meet Grant's Union army. Grant was concentrating his strength at Shiloh, Tennessee, and here the two armies would clash.

No one could possibly know what was about to happen. Shiloh would be the first large battle in the Western Theater, and out of this conflict would come carnage that the American public never dreamed possible. The people of both North and South were unprepared for the horrendous losses both armies would suffer: over 25,000 men wounded, killed, or missing. Both Southern and Union medical corps would face new challenges that would stimulate the development of new surgical and medical procedures in order to save lives.

An article from the <u>Memphis Daily Appeal</u> dated May 2, 1862, reported, "There were 1,200 patients in the hospitals, in addition to convalescents being cared for in private homes."[9] The slaughter at Shiloh accounted for part of this number; they were arriving by rail, straining the city's capacity to care for the wounded. The Memphis newspaper <u>The Avalanche</u> reported, "Many of the men had arrived in Memphis in a dying condition from having lain unattended on the battlefield in the cold rain." Memphis was not the only city that was struggling to save the lives of the bloodied Confederate soldiers who fell at Shiloh. After the battle some 5,000 maimed and crippled Southern troops and Northern prisoners were evacuated to Corinth, Mississippi. "Citizens of Corinth were horrified at the ghastly spectacle as the trains of army wagons lumbered in from the battlefield dripping blood from their heaped up piles of groaning, suffering wounded. Maimed and suffering men lay everywhere, on porches, on sidewalks, on platforms of railroad stations."[10] After Shiloh the medical professions, both North and South, realized they were unprepared to handle the mental anguish, misery, and suffering that the modern battlefields produced.

Beauregard had anticipated that he would have to retreat from his fortifications at Corinth and take his armies south to form a defensive line along the Mobile and Ohio Railroad. Under pressure from General Henry Halleck's buildup of Federal forces, their strength concentrated above Corinth, he hastily evacuated.

When the River brigades at Fort Randolph and Fort Pillow were ordered to evacuate, it was just a matter of time before Memphis would fall into Federal hands because the garrison there would soon be cut off from the main body of Confederate forces that were concentrating along the Mobile and Ohio Railroad.

Isaacs wrote that during this period there was confusion because the Southern armies had to leave Corinth quickly. The little community of Guntown, located below Corinth, had a hospital where wounded Confederate soldiers were being treated after the evacuation. At the time, Isaacs was assigned to Company D, 11th Arkansas Infantry.[11] He was the primary physician in charge of the hospital at Guntown, Mississippi, for a brief time - from May to June of 1862.

It wasn't a pleasant task to be a field surgeon, whether in the Southern army or Northern army, during the Civil War. They operated under the most primitive conditions. If a hospital was not available, a home or a barn might do. Often a site was chosen for a field hospital near a stream or river to ensure an adequate supply of water. The field hospital had to be close to the battlefield itself so the wounded could be transported there quickly. A lot of death and destruction occurred in northwestern Mississippi where

Isaacs was stationed. Northwestern Mississippi would be bitterly fought over throughout the length of the conflict between the states, and doctors would be hard pressed to take care of the wounded in this theater. The Federal forces would continue to hold the larger cities of importance, using them as bases of operations against the countryside. This part of Mississippi would be called Forrest's Country because the Confederate general Nathan Bedford Forrest held the countryside and the Union occupied Memphis. Not only would Memphis be used as a staging area by the Federals, it would also be used as a hospital base.

Isaacs and other physicians had many duties assigned to them during the Civil War. They were responsible for the establishment of hospitals that would accommodate the sick and the wounded. Equipment and medical supplies had to be ordered for the transportation of the sick and wounded from the battlefield to the hospital. This was one of many duties the army surgeon struggled with during the war. The responsibility of keeping and preserving accurate medical records was necessary because the government would have to depend on them for the future pension system it would provide. Upon the surgeon's shoulders rested the accuracy of these records that would insure disabled veterans compensation for the contributions and sacrifices they made for their country. The Civil War established a set of standards of organization that would become a prototype that would influence all future armies worldwide.

Many doctors in both the North and South who entered the medical service during the war were already successful in their civilian practices. This was true of Isaacs. Before he enlisted in the Confederate services he had a successful practice in Saline County.

The medical practices they brought with them during this period gave little regard for the cleaning of wounds and sterilization of surgical equipment. The surgeons knew little about the side effects of cruel drugs that they used, such as opium, morphine, and other harmful chemicals. In spite of their lack of knowledge, the Civil War advanced the medical profession. This was reflected in the saving of soldiers' lives who were wounded in battle.

The mortality rate associated with the injury compared with other armies before the Civil War was significantly reduced. A successful method for treating gangrene was developed by Dr. Middleton Goldsmith, Surgeon, USA. "While the patient was under anesthesia, the sloughing tissue was dissected out with forceps, the wound edges were painted with bromide, and the wound was then packed with cotton lint soaked in a very mild bromide solution. Bromide, which is a strong irritant, burned away the dead tissue and promoted healing through the granulation of healthy tissue."[12] Doctors observed that segregation of the wounded helped to prevent the spread of infectious diseases. This was before Louis Pasteur presented scientific proof of the bacterial origin of diseases in 1876-1877.

Pioneering ideals were put in place out of necessity. At Shiloh Dr. Irwin used field tents, arranging them in rows to care for the wounded. This would become a standard practice throughout the war, and because of his ideal the field hospital was born which both North and South used. The conflict produced physicians who came out of the war far more knowledgeable concerning anatomy, surgical techniques, and trauma diagnosis and able to apply new techniques developed by advanced surgical dexterity in treating injury.

Surgeons from both the North and South had to deal with trauma that was never before experienced on such a large scale up to that time. The one ounce conical ball fired from a musket was capable of shattering, splitting and splattering a long bone on impact. It was because of this that surgeons treating these frightful injuries learned early in the war that amputation of a limb or an arm was the best means of saving a soldier's life.[13] Future planners of human destruction would design the steel jacket projectile of a smaller caliber that would make a cleaner wound and offer a more humane death.

The Civil War soldier faced a variety of new weapons that were developed during the war designed to kill an opponent more efficiently. The repeating rifle developed toward the end of the Civil War by the Union army gave a soldier the ability to fire more rapidly without reloading after every shot. The lever action repeating rifle increased the firepower on the battlefield and caused dread in the Confederate forces when they went up against this weapon. The rifle cannon demonstrated its ability to penetrate masonry fortifications during the Union bombardment at Fort Pulaski, South Carolina. The Merrimac and the Monitor were forerunners of modern battleships that would play decisive roles in future wars. Heavy caliber naval guns protected by iron sheeting were mounted on ironclads and would spell doom to wooden ships. The submarine was developed and torpedoes were introduced to warfare. The Gattling Gun appeared on the battlefield and had the ability to dispense a seemingly endless rain of bullets against an enemy. This type of weapon would evolve into the machine gun, which would become the ultimate killing machine, causing millions of casualties during World War I.

These new technologies created a killing field. Weapons firing lead projectiles and artillery filled with canister would cut down large formations of men marching elbow to elbow in Napoleonic-style linear formations. These weapons obliterated bone, causing horrible flesh wounds. The physician had to care for the wounded and dying as the battle raged with fury. The air would be filled with the thunder of artillery, the clash of arms, and the screaming of canister as it passed overhead.

In a letter to her cousin, a woman living at Ripley, Mississippi, described the horror she witnessed after the retreat of the crippled Southern army from Corinth, Mississippi.

"I now come to a part of my story, cousin, so horrible that my fainting heart almost stands still when I recall it. Our retreating army left here in hospitals large numbers of wounded without medical attention or provisions and but few nurses. The care of the poor fellows fell heavily on the few in the distracted state of the town, Sister Martha and myself, principally, we being the nearest. We did the best we could for them, sent them clothes and bedclothes and cooked for them, but the Yankee ruffians would often snatch it from the stove before it was done.

"I seized a moment one day when none of the ruffians were in my house or yard and ran down to the hospital to see if I could not do something for the poor fellows, and O, my God, may I never more behold such a sight! The two rooms were crowded; the bare, hard, bloodstained floor was so nearly covered that I could scarcely pass between their miserable pallets. A few were on cots. Here lay a poor fellow shot through the lungs, every breath he drew almost a death pang, there a poor little smooth-faced, curly hair boy almost 17 years old, with his knee and arm shattered, moaning piteously; some with their arms just cut off, some with their legs off, others wounded in every imaginable part. I spoke a few trembling, horrified words to some I passed, until I came to a poor boy shot through the bowels, who was in his last agonies, and giving vent to his dying thoughts in broken words and moans and none to listen to him. I could brave it no longer, my woman's heart failed me, and I sank on the blood-begrimed floor by his side, crying fit to kill myself, offering such words of sympathy, comfort, and consolation as rose to my lips from my full heart."[14]

She was describing in language of that era what she witnessed: terrible emotional traumas and destruction to the human anatomy on a mass scale never before seen, caused by the introduction of canister, grapeshot, and exploding shells on the modern battlefield, which were used during the siege of Corinth on October 3-4 of 1862.

It wasn't this awesome presentation of deadly weapons on the battlefield that created the most devastation during the course of the war, however. The deadliest adversary that every soldier faced during the Civil War was an ancient enemy called disease. Outbreaks of measles, smallpox, malaria, pneumonia, dysentery, typhoid, and a general ignorance of what caused diseases would cause two-thirds of the casualties. This period in American history was void of any recognition of one of the basic causes of diseases.

Poor sanitation practices were expected as normal, and personal hygiene was far from the minds of most soldiers.

Doctors were not immune to the many infections and diseases that they were exposed to while treating the sick and the wounded. Out of lack of knowledge, their disregard for personal hygiene exposed them to many of these diseases. I believe this was a case with Isaacs, for soon after he established the hospital at Guntown, he was compelled to resign his commission as surgeon in the Confederate army because of illness.

Tupelo, Mississippi, June 19, 1862

Sir,
"I hereby tender my immediate and unconditional resignation as surgeon in the Confederate States. My reasons are long in dysfunction and now as frilly declining health."

Very respectfully
You're obedient servant
James L. Isaacs
Surgeon, Confederate States Army

To Doctor H. S. Hourd
Surgeon and Medical Doctor

"Surgeon James L. Isaacs having applied for a certificate of disability to which I grant a discharge from the service. I certify that I have carefully examined the said surgeon James L. Isaacs and find him to be laboring under general derangement of his system, severe fever and slight jauntiest. Which unfits him for the performance of the reparable duties of a surgeon in the Army. He is 36 years old, and shows the effects on his person of recent disease. I hereby recommend that he be discharged from the service."

Tupelo, Mississippi, June 18, 1862, B. M. Mtle. Surgeon C. S. A.[15]

My wife, Deborah Reynolds, summed up this chapter clearly when she wrote, "Under these atrocious conditions of death and disease, I think of heroism. Who were the heroes of this war? Were the generals, such as Lieutenant General Nathan Bedford Forrest or General Grant who led his troops into battle to capture and defeat the enemy? Were the field doctors, such as James Isaacs, who used their skills in primitive conditions trying to med men with wounds that were almost unbearable for the eye to see? Was it the soldiers that fought so gallantly for their country? The men that were so far from home, the men that marched with worn shoes and that riskedtheir lives with each day of battle? A man becomes a hero in different ways. I think every man that served i this long, deadly war was a hero in his own right foreach one of us who lives inthis great contry tda.

CHAPTER 4

Retreat from Corinth and The Battle of Iuka

After the evacuation of Fort Pillow, the 18th was ordered below Corinth, Mississippi.[1] By the time the regiment reached Mississippi, General Beauregard had withdrawn the Confederate army from Corinth and formed a line of defenses protecting the Mobile and Ohio Railroads.

Prior to the Southern retreat from Fort Pillow, a large Union buildup had taken place and was positioned north of the city waiting for orders to attack the Confederates. Beauregard's numbers were quickly being depleted because of sickness. Realizing he couldn't be reinforced and knowing he had little time to withdraw, it was only a matter of time before his army would be overwhelmed by General Halleck's superior numbers. On May 25, 1862, he called his officers in to discuss how to evacuate the city and safely slip out without the Federals knowing he was leaving. A plan was devised to secretly remove the troops on the night of the 29th by creating a diversion. The railroad leading south was still intact and in Confederate possession. The plans were to evacuate the army by rail and deceive the Union into believing Beauregard was being reinforced. When a train would leave with troops and equipment, the Confederates would cheer loudly as though they were being reinforced. This was repeated throughout the night, and by morning Hallack was convinced that the Confederates were about to launch an offensive against his front. The sound of steam whistles and the rhythmic click-clack of locomotive cars passing over the rails must have rattled his nerves because he ordered Grant to be held in reserve and to be ready to reinforce him when the attack came.

Colonel John N. Daly commanded the 18[th2], which was assigned to General Braxton Bragg's command, Army of the Mississippi, Third Division, commanded by Brigadier General Dabney H. Maury. On arriving, the 18th Infantry's dilemma with the weather, which wasn't cooperating, continued. Constant rains fell, soaking clothes, bedding, and personal gear, which added to their misery. Water pits were dug around the camp as a source of drinking water, creating a natural breeding ground for disease. Because of these unsanitary conditions, sickness continued to take its toll on the regiment.

General Sterling Price had accepted command of the District of Tennessee with orders to protect the Confederate lines of communication, keeping the Mobile and Ohio Railroad open.[3] Evidently Price was not happy to be in Mississippi. Bragg was his superior, which added to his frustration, because Bragg's plans for advancing into Tennessee were unclear. Price wanted to be placed in command of the trans-Mississippi District. His dissatisfaction was deep-rooted. He was from Missouri and felt the state was left unprotected after the Confederate high command ordered his troops transferred to Mississippi. Price tried to rectify his dilemma by making a trip to the Confederate capital at Richmond, Virginia; he was hoping to persuade President Davis into giving him permission to transfer the Missouri troops back to the trans-Mississippi District. Davis wanted his request submitted in writing, and after several days sent for the general to discuss the proposal with him. The president told Price that he would have to remain in Mississippi. Price informed the president that he would submit a written resignation and return to his native Missouri to raise another army and "fight again under the flag of Missouri and win victories for the South in spite of the government."[4]

Grant called him "Old Woodpecker" because a woodpecker has the ability to mislead its enemies. Price was also determined like a woodpecker to drill holes in the enemy's defenses if he was given the opportunity to peck in Missouri. He had fought in the Mexican war and proved at Lexington, Kentucky, that he could take entrenched troops protected by earthen works. But he made the mistake of being arrogant about his successes in Kentucky to Beauregard while on inspection of the recently rebuilt works outside Corinth. He boasted, "Well, these things may be fine; I never saw anything of the kind but once, and then I took them." This is one of the reasons he was not popular with the politicians in Richmond. Price was originally from Virginia and was popular in the state, especially with the press who were looking for a tough and ready-to-fight general who would end the stalemate at Corinth. Price was not a West Point graduate. The politicians, especially President Davis, didn't trust anyone in the army who was not an alumnus of the military academy. In order to be heard in Richmond, you had to be a member of this elite fraternity. They felt that Price was not a gentleman, but only some backwoodsman who commanded nothing more then a mob of rough frontiersmen.

Upon returning to Tupelo on July 2, 1862, Bragg placed Price in command of the Army of the West and gave him the responsibility of defending the District of Tennessee. Bragg was not in favor of weakening the Confederate defenses that protected a line of defenses stretching from Tupelo to Vicksburg, Mississippi, and agreed with Davis that Price should remain in the state for the time being. After assuming command, he began consolidating units which had been placed on picket duty and were scattered about the countryside, protecting the approaches to the Confederate bases along the Mobile and Ohio Railroad. Price began organizing these fragmented forces in order to form a single-effect fighting force, concentrating his newly formed army at Tupelo, Mississippi. During the reorganization, the 18th was assigned to the Army of the West, Major General Sterling Price commanding, Maury's Division, and assigned to General William L. Cabell's Brigade.

The new assignment didn't improve the weather, which would continue to plague the regiment, turning hot and dry later in the summer. In spite of the bad weather, the troops made good use of their time while in camp. An article written by Colonel Thomas L. Snead entitled <u>With Price East of the Mississippi</u> gives a good description of preparations being made for future actions. Part of this article was dated August 11, 1862, which gives us an historical reference point revealing the time frame in which these events were occurring.Price didn't return from Richmond empty-handed; while there he had procured supplies for his army. Even though there were hot words exchanged between Davis and himself, the trip and efforts were not without reward; he brought back arms, equipment and ample clothing along with commissaries to feed his troops. Bragg was especially impressed with General Lewis Henry Little's division and made the comment on reviewing Price's troops, saying "The army, not only were these men well armed and equipped, well fed, well clothed, and well provided with everything that army in the field needed, but they were thoroughly organized, drilled and disciplined."[5] The troops were not idle, but were taking full advantage of their time, preparing themselves for the prime objective which was the reestablishment of a strong Confederate presence in Tennessee.

While in camp, writing letters back home by those who were fortunate enough to know how to read and write was an important part of their pastime. A large percentage of the Southern soldiers were yeomen and subsistence farmers from rural backgrounds. Many were highlanders from isolated mountain regions of the Ozarks and Appalachian ranges, and some could not read or write. Many of the sons from the planter caste were more fortunate because their families had the financial resources to educate them.

Those who could write must have helped those who couldn't compose letters to loved ones back home or to a person in the community who could read. News of the events that were happening in the lives of George Isaacs, Stockton and McGuire since being assigned to posts in Tennessee and Mississippi was reaching home also by newspapers and by those returning from the front. I do not have the details of what they wrote; perhaps they reassured their loved ones that all would be well in spite of the hardships they were enduring. Possibly they wrote about the miserable weather they were having in Mississippi. Maybe they wrote about a good sermon they heard preached in camp or about their struggle to secure Southern independence; politics was a big issue in camp. Religious services were common both in the Northern and Southern armies. It wasn't uncommon for pastors to serve as both commander and preacher in the Confederate and Union armies.

On September 1, 1862, Bragg sent a telegram to Price instructing him to watch Major General William Starke Rosecrans and prevent his Union army from joining forces with Don Carlos Buell in middle Tennessee. Bragg was engaging the enemy in Tennessee and wanted the Army of the West to move north, but left the details to Price on how to achieve this goal. Bragg wrote, "Buell's whole force is in retreat upon Nashville, destroying their stores; watch Rosecrans and prevent a junction, or if he escapes you, follow him closely."[6] This was the opportunity Price was hoping for. He had been waiting for an opportunity to test Rosecrans' resolve to defend the river landing on the Tennessee at Eastport, 35 miles east of Corinth.

On September 11, 1862, Price's Army of the West moved out of its Guntown and Baldwyn area camps, which were located along the Mobile and Ohio Railroad north of Tupelo, Mississippi, and marched toward the town of Iuka, Mississippi. On September 13, Price arrived at Iuka, located 20 miles east of Corinth, Mississippi, only to find that the town had been abandoned by the 18th Wisconsin under the command of Colonel Robert Murphy. The Confederate armies began to fortify their positions in anticipation of a Union countermove calculated to prevent Price from entering middle Tennessee and linking up with Bragg. Or would he attack Corinth? Major General Ulysses S. Grant was Rosecrans' superior and both were puzzled why Price had marched to Iuka and were trying to guess what his true objective was. They knew that he was close enough to threaten Corinth from the northeast. Major General Earl Van Dorn's army could attack Corinth by marching north from Ripley and then launching a two frontal attack on the fortification there. Grant wrote, "Having satisfied myself that Van Dorn could not reach Corinth under four days with an army embracing all arms, I determined to leave Corinth with a force sufficient to resist cavalry and to attack at Iuka."[7]

On the 19th, Price had positioned Maury's and Little's divisions in a line of battle northwest of Iuka, covering the Brownsville Road. Hebert's brigade was drawn out of Little's division and held in reserve in case the enemy threatened at a different point. About 2 p.m. that afternoon, pickets placed on the Jacinto Road were driven in and reported that the enemy was advancing in force. Price was expecting Rosecrans to march out of Corinth, or approach northwest, and travel down the Burnsville Road and then attack Iuka. Anticipating this move, Price had concentrated the main body of his army northwest of the town.

On hearing that his pickets had been driven in, he realized that Grant had set a trap. Grant had divided his command, sending Major General Edward O. C. Ord down the Burnsville Road and Rosecrans on the Jacinto Road. Rosecrans was to get as close as possible without being detected and then turn north, launching an attack from the two southern approaches to the city. Grant had planned to open two fronts and simultaneously attack the Confederates when the two armies had positioned themselves north and south of the city, leaving the Army of the West with no means of escaping.[8]

The Confederates were now facing two hostile forces that were fast closing on them from two different directions. Before the Army moved out of Guntown, Little pleaded with Price, urging him not to move against Iuka. He heatedly argued with Price and tried to persuade him that the absence of the Army would be an open invitation for a Union counter thrust into the interior of Mississippi. Old Woodpecker had gotten himself into a dangerously tight spot and was about to get his feathers plucked by two Union hands that were intent on squeezing the life out of him.

Price ordered Little to send Hebert's brigade, which had been held in reserve, to engage the enemy and check his advance until his strength could be determined. No one had expected the enemy to outflank Price. Hebert's men were wondering how the Yankees had slipped past the cavalry which was supposed to be screening the southern approaches to the city. Price had neglected to secure his southern flank and personally should have done more to make sure it was better screened. Armstrong's cavalry had been sent out on patrol, but his resources were spread too thinly. Even though Armstrong had to gather reconnaissance on both fronts, the ultimate responsibility for failure fell on Price's shoulders for not covering the Jacinto Road beyond Barnett's Crossroads. Hebert had been positioned behind the Confederate lines that were facing Ord. Hebert had about 1,774 men in his brigade plus 1,600 men of Martin's brigade that were sent forward to reinforce Hebert.[9] These numbers would prove to be inadequate to dislodge Rosecrans' threat from the south, and their absence would weaken Price's ability to defend the threat from Ord.

Hebert wrote in his report, "On the 19th, up to about 3:00 p.m., the division was in line of battle on the Brownsville road, with the exception of Second Brigade [Hebert's], which was halted near the line, ready to move to any threatened point. At that hour it received orders to proceed forthwith to the Bay Springs road, south of the town, to check the enemy, reported to be advancing in that direction very rapidly and in strong force. The brigade met him three-quarters of a mile from town, and quickly forming line of battle, not only checked his advance, but drove him from the advantageous positions he had already occupied. Here it became evident that the brigade unsupported could not drive back the superior numbers before it. Soon, however, the Fourth Brigade appeared on the field, and Little took command of the troops present."[10] Major General Price at that point personally took charge. The engagement continued until there was no light left, and both armies bivouacked for the night.

Rosecrans had intended to divide his army into two columns, Brigade General David Sloane Stanley moving up the Fulton Road and Brigade General Charles Smith Hamilton up the Jacinto Road, but changed his mind when he realized that the distance Stanley would have to travel was farther than first calculated in order to reach the intersections of the Fulton and Tuscumbia roads at Cartersville. The confusion was further compounded when Stanley became uncertain of how to execute Rosecrans' orders after reaching Cartersville. Both columns had to be in position and be close enough to support each other during the initial attack on Iuka. Because of the delay, Rosecrans was doubtful that the two columns would be in position. He recalled Stanley and sent both columns up the Jacinto Road. The decision to regroup would later prove to be a blunder, for it left the door wide open for Old Woodpecker to flee the nest, down the Fulton Road.

When the Southern army first made contact with the vanguard of Rosecrans' forces, Ord was waiting. His advance guard was located seven miles above the Confederate lines and on alert, listening for the first sound of cannon and musket fire that would signal for him to attack and engage the Rebels. Grant had not heard from Rosecrans and felt that he was farther away from Iuka than he actually was. Consequently, Ord did not engage simultaneously when the first elements of Rosecrans' army were challenged by Hebert. The delay and confusion saved Price's army. There is no question that if Grant's original plan had been fully implemented and carried through, the outcome of the battle would have been much more favorable for the Yankees.

During the night, Maury and other officers met with Price and urged him to evacuate as soon as possible before morning. Maury argued that Grant was concentrating his army in overwhelming numbers and would attack in the morning, overwhelming their defenses, sweeping aside their cavalry, and then destroying their wagons and trains. Price was reluctant to give up the fight and felt confident they would be able to defeat the enemy in the morning. With all his chief officers dead set against any further

32

hostilities, "He reluctantly directed them to carry out the orders which had been issued the preceding morning for withdrawal of the army to Baldwyn."[11] That night a courier from Van Dorn's staff brought a dispatch urging Price to hurry and meet him for a joint venture against the enemy. This message gave Price a way out; he was torn between the sane advice of his officers and the hard reality of a looming, total defeat. Fortunately for the brave who were about to die, he chose sanity.

Those units that were heavily engaged at Iuka were especially discouraged because of the losses they suffered, and they knew they were leaving behind their friends and comrades who were still lying on the battlefield and in the woods south of town. In addition to those who were killed, 200 sick soldiers were left in town and on the road.

The retreat was done quickly as possible; consequently, the Confederates didn't have time to bury their dead. Captain Benjamin Jett of the 17th Arkansas wrote, "Our Troops slept on the battle-field 'mid' the groans of the wounded and dying, and the corpses of the dead."[12,13] Leaving the carnage behind and knowing that their enemy would bury their dead, with downcast faces that had been blackened and stained by gunpowder, they traveled south. Their uniforms were coated with mud from recent rains that had turned the roads into a quagmire of mud. Some of their shirts were splattered with the blood of friend and foe. Demoralized and weary, they trudged on through the countryside on the way to Baldwyn, scavenging the fields and gardens for something edible to eat. The proud, disciplined army that had marched out of their camps just a few short days ago had at that time been admirably complimented by General Bragg. He felt that they were well prepared to take on anything. There was no question about their fighting ability; they had proven they could fight and aggressively attack General Sanford, drive the Yankees back and regain the ground they lost. The question that was going through their minds must have been, "Will we be morally and physically fit to fight another day?"

Maury's troops were not engaged in the thick of the fight. During the retreat, his fresh troops were used as a rear guard and helped prevent Rosecrans from pursuing the fleeing, fragmented units that had suffered heavy battle casualties. Maury would later be chosen to fulfill a similar role at Davis Bridge during the retreat from the Siege of Corinth and was very instrumental in saving Price's and Van Dorn's armies from total annihilation.

Maury was levelheaded and presented a good argument in favor of evacuating the city. He was placed in the rear with the responsibility of preventing Rosecrans from pursuing and overtaking Price's main body during the retreat. Price had heavily relied upon Little for advice; Little was killed during the engagement at Iuka. He trusted Maury's judgment and would rely on it in the future. Maury wrote, "At 2 o'clock in the morning orders were given to move off the baggage and to withdraw the army from its position. Phifer's brigade was sent in advance with the train and I was ordered to cover the movements of the army with Cabell's and Barry's brigades. By daylight I had taken position with these brigades on the heights east of the town. The train and the army marched past me, and by order of the general commanding, I withdrew from my position at 8 a.m. and marched in rear of the army. The enemy followed us feebly, with cavalry chiefly, which was held in check all the time by the cavalry under General Armstrong, covering my rear.

"About 2 p.m., while halted at a point about 8 miles from Iuka, the pursuing enemy was drawn into an ambuscade, admirably planned and executed by General Armstrong, Colonel Rogers, and Captain Bledsoe. They received the fire of the Second Texas Sharpshooters; of Bledsoe's battery, with canister, at short range; were charged by McCulloch's cavalry, and were utterly routed. Our loss was 1 killed and 3 wounded. Theirs was of necessity much greater. During the remainder of the march to this place they ventured within range no more.

"I arrived here at dark on the 22d. The troops have without exception conducted themselves on every occasion as disciplined soldiers."[14] The 18th Arkansas Infantry was not engaged during the fight, and possibly the only discomfort they suffered with was sore feet. Before they left their camps along the Ohio and Mobile Railroad, Maury's division was supplied with new shoes, and by the time they reached their objective, their feet were sore and blistered along with other units in Maury's command. After serving well during the retreat (they were part of Cabell's brigade), with painfully tender feet, wearily they retreated back to their bases at Baldwyn, arriving on the 23rd.

This was a bloody battle and Price suffered more than 700 casualties; some historians believe the numbers were much higher. Some of his officers must also have been discouraged over the losses, because they didn't enforce discipline, which was no excuse for Price's army reverting to a marauding mob on their retreat through the countryside. Little had been killed during the afternoon of the 19th, which must have added to their grief. The Army of the West was well equipped before they left their bases, but they returned with little to show for all the hard work and effort they had employed. They were eager for a Confederate victory, and it must have been disheartening, for the battle resulted in a Confederate loss that should have been a disaster.

They were totally exhausted from their ordeal, and with little energy or enthusiasm, they abandoned all military protocol, pitching what tents they had left and lying down with no regular camp plan, questioning in their minds if they would be ready for another brilliant tactical maneuver lead by Old Woodpecker.[15]

These events set the stage for one of the bloodiest battles to be fought in Mississippi, the objective being to secure the strategic railhead at Corinth.

CHAPTER 5

Fighting on Home Ground

All the principal characters of this story had lived in northern Mississippi and Alabama before the war and were familiar with this part of the state. They were now preparing to fight on home ground and in familiar territory. Perhaps this explains why the fighting was so ferocious by the Confederates during the Battle of Corinth. Not only were they familiar with the country, but also many Mississippi regiments participated in the battle, reinforcing the determination to hold native soil.

After leaving Fort Pillow, Lieutenant George W. Isaacs was stationed at Camp Priceville near Tupelo, Mississippi, along the Mobile and Ohio Railroad.[1] At the time of his enlistment Isaacs was 22 years old and was looking forward to a promising future studying law. This was disrupted and put on hold when he entered the service. He was elected second lieutenant in another company while still serving in Company B, First Arkansas Mounted Rifle. No doubt this was because of his active involvement in recruiting friends and relatives to help form Company H. He received his commission as a second lieutenant in the 18th Arkansas Infantry Regiment after the Battle of Oak Hills, Missouri.

Isaacs was born in Pickens County, Alabama, and left there when he was about 2 years old. His boyhood years were spent living in Marshall County, Mississippi. He was about 11 years old when the 1850 Census of Marshall County, Mississippi, was taken and was enumerated in that census, living in the household of his father, Silas Isaacs.[2] The early years there must have been happy times, making trips to Holly Springs with his parents. Holly Springs is the county seat. In early America the county seat was the center of social activities.

His parents must have encouraged him to study and gain knowledge while living near Holly Springs. The town was a center of education with several colleges established there before the Civil War, and in this atmosphere of learning George must have thrived. Holly Springs would become a staging ground and supply depot for Confederate armies operating in Mississippi in the early part of the war and headquarters for General Earl Van Dorn's army. It is more than probable that Isaacs made trips to visit friends at Holly Springs while stationed at Ripley.

The Holly Springs area played a significant role in influencing and shaping the lives of the Isaacs family. They were attracted there by opportunities to further educate the family, for economical reasons, and for the prospects of productive farmland - the same incentives that compelled pioneering families to push west. In the 1840's and 1850's northern Mississippi was a frontier and open to settlement during this period. They came there from Alabama with great hopes and expectations, hoping for a better tomorrow. This was what motivated most pioneer families to move, hoping for a new beginning.

The Isaacs' life in Marshall County was apparently productive and not a disappointment to them, especially the younger Isaacs who were nurtured and established there. Granville McGuire was listed in the 1850 Census of Marshall County, living with his father, Isaac McGuire.[3] The enumeration lists his father's occupation as a farmer born in Georgia, age 42. Grandville would marry Naomi J. Isaacs one year later on June 19, 1851, in Marshall County. Margaret Y. Isaacs would later marry Dr. Williams C. Gillespie in Saline County, Arkansas, on December 17, 1868. William Gillespie was enumerated as a being 5 years old at the time of the 1850 census and living in the household of his father in Marshall, County.[4] Also Margaret Y. Isaacs was reported on that same census as being 5 years old.[5] Elizabeth J. Isaacs, my second great grandmother, probably met my second great grandfather, Hartwell Stain Reynolds, in Marshall County, Mississippi, during that period. Hartwell's father, Henry Reynolds, was listed in the 1840 Census of Marshall County. The Reynolds family and Isaacs family must have been acquainted with one another, because they immigrated to Arkansas about the same period. Both families made purchases of land along the Saline River in Arkansas, settling within 30 miles of each other. To add even more to the significance of this area, Richard T. Stockton was born in Alabama. It is more than probable that he met Martha L. Isaacs in Mississippi, and they were later married in Saline County on September 5, 1860. All the Isaacs children were listed in the 1850 Census of Marshall County. I am sure that all three men were thinking about the events that shaped their early lives in Marshall County before the war began.

CHAPTER 6

The Siege of Corinth

Major General Earl Van Dorn, then headquartered at Holly Springs, made arrangements with General Price, after Price sent him a letter in late September proposing that they meet at Ripley, to begin the process of combining their commands. Van Dorn wrote, "On the 25th day of the same month (September) I received a dispatch by courier from General Price, stating that he was at Baldwyn and was then ready to join me with his forces in an attack on Corinth, as had been previously suggested by me."[1] Prior to this communication he had received a dispatch from Price in which he suggested that they come together and cooperate with each other. Van Dorn wrote, "On August 30 I received a dispatch from General Bragg, informing rite that he was about to march into Kentucky and would leave to General Price and myself the enemy in West Tennessee.

"On September 4, I received a communication from General Price, in which was enclosed a copy of the dispatch from General Bragg, above named, making an offer to co-operate with me."[2] The proposal to combine the two armies had tentatively been suggested prior to Prices' advance on Iuka, but didn't materialize until Van Dorn was given supreme command over the two armies.

Price wrote, "Having arranged with Major-General Van Dorn to unite my forces with his for active operations I joined him at Ripley on the 27th ultimo. My force at this time consisted of 10,498 effective infantry, 2,437 effective cavalry, 928 effective artillerymen, and 44 guns, including two 24-pounder howitzers and four rifled pieces of 3 5/8 caliber."[3] The union of the two forces was completed on September 28, 1862, bringing the fighting strength to about 22,000 men.

Grant and Rosecrans were closely watching the buildup of Confederate troops in the Ripley area and quickly began responding to this threat. Grant's reconnaissance was reporting these movements, and because of this he began to reinforce the Union army at Corinth, increasing its strength 23,000 men. By doing so he had correctly solved the puzzle and saved Rosecrans from impending defeat, for it was the Confederacy's intention to take the fortified railhead of Corinth.[4]

On or before September 28, 1862, a war council was held to determine the best strategy for an effective and decisive attack upon the fortifications. From the book <u>Battles and Leaders of the Civil War</u>, Volume 2, Page 742, Van Dorn gives his reasons for choosing this objective. "Surveying the whole field of operations before me, the conclusion forced itself irresistibly upon my mind that the taking of Corinth was a condition precedent to the accomplishment of anything of importance in west Tennessee. To take Memphis would be to destroy an immense amount of property without any adequate military advantage, every admitting that he could be held without heavy guns against the enemy's guns and mortar boats. A line of fortifications around Bolivar is intersected by the Hatchie River rendering it impossible to take them by quick assault. It was clear to my mind that if a successful attack could be made upon Corinth from the west and north-west, the forces there driven back to Tennessee and cut off, Bolivar and Jackson would easily fall, and then, upon the arrival of exchange prisoners of war, west Tennessee would soon be in our possession, and communication with General Bragg effected through middle Tennessee."[5]

It must have also been pointed out in this war council the national significance and strategic importance of the two railroads that crossed paths there. At Corinth, the Mobile and Ohio Railroad, and the Memphis and Charleston Railroad joined. This connected the Confederacy from the Mississippi to the Atlantic Ocean and to the Gulf of Mexico and north to Columbus, Kentucky on the Mississippi.

On the morning of September 29, 1862, the combined armies under the command of Van Dorn marched out of Ripley in the direction of Pocahontas, Mississippi. This movement was intended to create an illusion that an attack was coming against Bolivar, Tennessee, thus diverting Grant's attention from the true objective. The march was exceptionally hard on the troops because the weather was oppressively hot. In one of Van Dorn's reports, he describes the parched, dry country they were passing through. They were having a hard time replenishing their water supplies as they moved north. The army was made up of three divisions: Lovell's, Maury's, and Hebert's. Because of the large number of troops traveling over dirt roads, clouds of dust made it hard to breathe in the heat. With these conditions, it couldn't have been more difficult to move troops, much less surprise the enemy.

Van Dorn describes the order of march on October 3, 1862: "At day break on the third, the march resumed, Lovell's division, in front, kept the road on the south side of the Memphis and Charleston Railroad. Price, after marching on the same road about 5 miles, turned to left, crossing a railroad, and formed lines of battle in front of the outer line of entrenchments in and about 3 miles from Corinth."[6] The three divisions were now positioning themselves for the first attack upon the fortifications. The strategy for taking Corinth was kept secret from the rank and file and only made known to a few high-ranking officers in Van Dorn's command. The plan was made known just before the attack in order to preserve the element of surprise.

While researching this book I have tried to reenact the thoughts and emotions of the period, hoping to make sense of why they fought and endured such atrocious conditions that were associated with death and disease. The question of why they left the comforts of wives, families, and communities that they loved, why they went to war, violently quarreling against their fellow Americans, is a question that is trying to be answered unto this day. I have struggled trying to understand through letters, articles and diaries written during the Civil War about this inquiry. These documents dealt with honor, freedom, defending their county, religious duty, and rites of passage into manhood as well as the negative emotions that played a roll in motivating Southern men to persevere under such hardships. Reverberating these deep emotions the officers might have reminded their men, especially in the individual companies, the reasons why they had come prepared to do battle. Lieutenant George W. Isaacs may have said something to this effect to Company H, 18th Arkansas Infantry, which he helped recruit and organize. "Men of Company H, on your shoulders rests the fate of our great Southern nation. We stand at a crossroads in time. What we do on the field of battle will be preserved in the memory of those we love and hold dear to our hearts. Even as I speak, history is unfolding. Let it not be recorded that we were slack in our duty to capture the great prize, to live as free men in an independent South, free of the usurping dominance of Yankee arrogance and subjugation by an alien culture.

"Almost all of you have volunteered for the service. Some of you who are present here I personally recruited for our just cause. Many of us have been sick since the evacuation of Fort Pillow; suffering hardships and miseries have further been intensified by the weather here in Mississippi. Homesickness has been our constant companion, and we all long to tell those that are dear to us how much we love them and long to see them.

"It is because of our sacrifices and that of our friends and families back home that it has become of the utmost importance that we take and secure Corinth. By doing this, we can restore and preserve the flow of commerce, which has nurtured and connected our great nation. Therefore, let us take Corinth, which shall be the keystone of many victories that will pave the way into Tennessee, and then take us home to those we love.

"General Bragg has entrusted to us the duty of protecting the Mobile and Ohio Railroad, which we have faithfully executed. Now we are being asked to do that which is greater. As we well know, the Memphis and Charleston

Railroad terminates at Charleston, South Carolina. This important junction connects our great country to the sea. Our cities of commerce and trade must be left unrestricted if we are to continue our struggle. The people of Mobile, Decatur, Chattanooga, Charleston, Savannah, and Richmond are welded together by these great roads. Our fellow citizens of these communities are prayerfully hoping that we might regain what is ours. Let us remember the words of President Davis, who has inspired us so often to renew such sacrifices as our fathers have made to the holy cause of constitutional liberty."

By early afternoon on October 3, the divisions of Lovell, Maury, and Hebert had fought their way to the old pre-existing Confederate earthen works that had been constructed by the Confederate army in an attempt to fortify and hold Corinth. There they met strong resistance that checked their advance. Van Dorn in his official report writes, "I saw with regret the sun sink behind the horizon as the last of our sharp shooters followed the retreating foe into his uttermost lines. One hour more of daylight and victory would have soothed our grief for the loss of the gallant dead who sleep on that lost but not dishonored field."[7]

Rosecrans, commander of the Union army, had a different version of the same story. According to his report he states, "I bewailed that lack of daylight, which would have brought Hamilton's fresh and gallant division on the Confederate left and rear. That hour of daylight was not to be had, and while the regretful Confederate general lay down in his bivouac, I assembled my four division commanders and arranged the dispositions for the fight of the next day."[8] The simple truth of the matter was that the Federals put up a strong resistance, in particular one hot-blooded Scotchman named MacArthur who commanded a brigade, who was the father of General Douglas MacArthur who commanded the American forces in the Pacific Theater during World War II.

Maury was a West Point graduate. He graduated 37th in a class of 59 from the U.S. Military Academy in 1846. He married the daughter of Matthew Fontaine Maury, a naval commander and scientist, who wrote the book Physical Geography of the Sea and Its Meteorology. Cabell graduated 33rd in a class of 44 from the U.S. Military Academy in 1850 and commanded the 18th Arkansas Infantry Regiment as well as other regiments in his division. Van Dorn and Lovell also graduated from the U.S. Military Academy. Lovell graduated with distinction in 1842, being ninth in his class. All these men were trained at the academy in Napoleonic tactics of warfare.

This type of warfare in its simplest form meant marching large groups of men shoulder to shoulder in massive formations, followed by more formations. As the first formations were cut down the second and third formations formed ranks, continuing the advance by sheer numbers until the opponent was overwhelmed. Van Dorn hoped to surprise the enemy and demonstrate this tactic with a massive attack, moving quickly across the battlefield, then overcome the Union defenses, crushing them completely.

It would be safe to assume that exhaustion and fatigue were now in command of the troops as they witnessed the last rays of light fading into darkness, signaling the end of the battle. As the darkness enveloped them, it reassured them that they would be able to replenish their strength in the comfort of its blanket. The relentlessly hot sun had tormented them as they fought their way to the utter works; their tormentor was now fading from their sight. In the cool night they would be safe from the sniper's bullet and the mouth of the cannon that awaited them at dawn. I'm sure some of them thought of a time long ago when they heard the voice of their mother calling, "Johnnie, it's time to go to bed," and remembered the comfort of her voice as she said, "I love you," and the warmth of her arms as she prayed, "Lord, watch over Johnnie Reb. Please keep him safe, and wake him in the morning light."

The sounds of the night gave way to the roar of the cannon as the Confederate batteries opened up at four o'clock in the morning, announcing the hostilities were beginning.[8] Wiping the sleep from their eyes they hurry about to make themselves ready for battle. Colonel Daly, commander of 18th Arkansas had been issued his orders for the day. He then consulted with his officers and reviewed the battle plans for that day. Lieutenant Isaacs and other officers on receipt of these orders passed the instructions to their companies. Hebert was to be placed on the left. This deployment was to be hidden from Yankee observation. Cabell's brigade was to be pulled out of Maury's division and placed behind on the left of Hebert's division. Maury's division was to hold the center and Lovell's division would be positioned on the right.[9] It's more than probable that Isaacs might have said to his company, "The ground we gained yesterday was paid for in full. Some of those that were with me yesterday are no longer here today. Let us not forget our sacrifices or those who placed their lives on the altars of liberty and paid for this ground we gained with their blood. I've never asked you to do anything that I am not willing to do or go anywhere that I wouldn't go. My sword shall be drawn as evidence of my resolve to lead you into battle. Follow me and may God's divine protection be with us."

CHAPTER 7

Into the Mouth of the Cannon

Confederate Assault on Union Fortifications at Corinth

Isaacs and the other officers waited for orders to advance. They knew that when the order came to march, it would be into the mouth of the cannon that awaited them. They would be facing on their right the three-gun redoubt of Battery Robinett and on their left Battery Powell, artillery blasting. The determined defenders were well positioned to deliver a deadly fire from all directions. It was October 4, and the morning was clear and oppressively hot by 9 a.m. with temperatures soaring to the mid 90s. By 10 a.m., skirmishing on Maury's front began to intensify and so did the heat.[1]

Perhaps the weather was signaling a bad omen reminiscent of the conditions that plagued their numbers that summer, thinning their ranks with sickness and disease. Misfortune must have been tied into their fate, because a key figure in the Confederate high command, General Louis Hebert, was sick, delaying their anticipated victory that morning. Throughout the summer, the air had been filled with rain and the sound of thunderstorms, hindering the preparation for this very moment. This time it was not the sound of thunder they heard as they advanced. Now it was the deafening roar of artillery and musketry, signaling the death and carnage that were about to come. It wasn't the rain that filled the air, for the morning had broken, revealing a clear sky. Now a different kind of atmosphere awaited them that morning. It was an atmosphere filled with the instruments of war, as the cannon filled with grapeshot belched destruction, and minie balls fired from muskets filled the air with a storm of rain.

The hot sun was no longer a worry, for the contestants were clothed in heavy smoke, concealing their movements. The first assault was by Green's left directed at Battery Powell. Observing these movements the defenders could see three or four assaulting columns of regiments probably a hundred yards apart, forming a front across the battlefield. As the smoke drifted between reloads of the guns, it revealed their positions. Onward they charged, seemingly oblivious to the fire that was being directed upon them, as sheets of fire leaped from guns and iron rained down on them at close range, for the advance started 600 yards from Corinth. Above the roar of the battle could be heard the rebel yell and the rhythmic shuffle of limb and foot in obedient unison as the columns rushed forward. Onward they rushed, resolved to fulfill their predetermined assignments as they faced horrendous fire that was plowing through their columns. Steadily they closed up the ranks to replace their fallen comrades who lay dead or wounded on an ever increasingly bloody field.

In spite of the furious discharge of grape and canister, a remnant of the First Missouri under Colonel Gates managed to storm the works of Battery Powell. Sergeant Payne of the Sixth Missouri witnessed and described the rain of destruction that was exploding through their ranks. "Not for a moment did they halt. Every instant death smote. It came in a hundred shapes, every shape a separate horror. Here a shell, short fused, exploding in the thinning ranks, would rend its victims and splatter their comrades with brains, flesh, and blood. Men's heads were blown to atoms. Fragments of human flesh still quivering alive would slap other men in the face, or fall to earth to be trampled under foot."[2]

Three assaulting columns were hurled against Batteries Robinett and Powell. It was on the last attack against Battery Powell Cabell's brigade was ordered to reinforce Colonel Gates. During this attack they experienced some of the heaviest fighting of the campaign, which left their ranks devastated. I can well imagine the intense anxiety that Isaacs and his company felt as they waited for the anticipated order to assist their comrades in the fight that started at 10 a.m. Cabell's brigade was being held in reserve on the west side of the Mobile and Ohio Railroad north of Corinth. It had been a long morning, for they had been ready to engage the enemy by 7 a.m. I am sure many were praying, "Yea, though I walk through the valley of the shadow of death, I will fear no evil: for thou art with me; thy rod and thy staff they comfort me."

Cabell wrote, "About 11 a.m. I received an order from General Maury, delivered by Captain Flowerree, adjutant-general, to move rapidly to the support of Colonel Gates, who had entered the enemy's breastwork and could not hold it for the want of ammunition. This order was received with a shout by the whole brigade, who had stood this terrible cannonading for more than an hour. I immediately after receiving the order moved, by the left flank at double-quick until I crossed the Mobile and Ohio Railroad. After crossing the railroad through a terrible fire of artillery I faced to the front and moved on the enemy's works, the left in the open field and the right and center through a skirt of woods about 50 yards wide, expecting to find the Missouri brigade. If this brigade had, however, fallen back, taking a road on my extreme right. Instead of meeting the Missouri brigade, as I had been informed I would, I found the enemy in line of battle just outside of the timber and about 300 yards in front of their breastworks. My left became engaged at once after facing to the front and the whole line in a few minutes afterward, when I gave the command to charge. As soon as the command was given the whole line moved at double-quick almost as one man, shouting 'Butler!'"[3]

Isaacs was aware of what he was about to face. I am sure the memory of the fight at Oak Hills, Missouri, must have been fresh on his mind. Over a year had passed since he had stood on another battlefield as a private waiting for the orders to advance. That order came from Colonel T. P. Churchill, commander of the First Regiment Arkansas Mounted Riflemen. When the order was received, Isaacs' mind and body must have switched from tension, born from his wait, to a readiness to fight. Earlier that morning during breakfast Union batteries had opened up on their regiment, forcing them to take cover and find protection in a wooded area. From there they moved toward Springfield, Missouri, and waited in a hollow.

Tension mounted in the hollow; finally an aide of General Sterling Price, commanding the Southern forces at Oak Hills, Missouri, brought the order instructing Churchill to reinforce Colonel Slack. Churchill's regiment did not hesitate and instantly moved in one accord amid a shower of incoming fire from the enemy. Isaacs was a green recruit at Oak Hills (Wilson Creek) and was about to experience the realities of modern warfare. His officers would order him, then a private, and others to charge into the face of death. He knew what it meant to march into the mouth of the cannon, for murderous fire in the form of grapeshot had left its mark on him. The hill his

45

regiment took was not paid without a heavy price, and he remembered that the outcome was uncertain and hung in the balance for several hours. An Iowa regiment of Union defenders hotly contested the dispute over ownership with unceasing volleys of musketry and well-positioned cannon fire.

If it were not for the encouragement from the officers and the example they set at Oak Hills, the regiment would have lost heart. Colonel Churchill wrote, "At times we would drive them up the hill, and in turn they would rally and cause us to fall back. At length we shouted a gallant charge and drove them over the hill."[4]

Isaacs waited in the woods with his company, reflecting on what had happened at Oak Hills. When the order came, the 18th Arkansas Infantry emerged from the woods at Corinth with the rest of the brigade. Much to their astonishment, they realized Battery Powell had been reinforced. As a private at Oak Hills, Isaacs had faithfully followed orders issued by the officers of his company. Isaacs would now ask others to follow him, and without hesitation the 18th Arkansas Company H complied with the whole command, for all were acting as one prepared for battle when they shouted "Butler!"

Captain Thrasher, an officer in Company D, 18th Arkansas, described the rain of terror that belched from the cannons. "In front of the works was an open space of about 250 yards, somewhat obstructed with logs and brush. Over this space we were ordered by General Cabell to charge at double-quick. A murderous storm of iron and leaden hail came down furiously upon us from the batteries, and as we advanced, volley after volley of musket balls, like the thickening blasts of a hurricane, swept the field."[5]

Through this storm the 18th Arkansas closed in on the right of the battery, as their ever-thinning ranks grew smaller. With his sword drawn, fulfilling his promise to his men not to waver in the face of the enemy, Isaacs was true to his word. He could be clearly seen out in front of his men as he advanced with other officers of the 18th Arkansas. Isaacs could see Daly at the head of the column, leading the company in the charge. Captain Parrish could also be seen, encouraging the men forward. Suddenly Colonel Daly was struck and fell back, lying mortally wounded on the field. Somewhere behind Isaacs, Stockton was advancing and must have observed this also. Again without warning, a projectile struck Parrish, wounding him. First Lieutenant John B. Walker would not be exempt from the deadly storm of iron and lead, for one of many shots struck him in the leg. Now his superior officer lay dead, and his second-in-command lay wounded. Isaacs was one of the few left to lead. This was his moment of truth that would clearly define the reason he fought. Raising his sword even higher he beckoned the few forward. His gesture of courage was soon stopped a bullet that severed three fingers, knocking his sword to the ground.

I wonder what was going on in Isaacs' mind. The impact of the projectile on his hand must have sent shock waves through his body. I know that in crisis the human body and mind can respond in strength and endurance beyond what is normal. What Isaacs did next goes beyond the understanding of the mind and transcends to that which is in the realm of the spirit. Knowing that the loss of blood from his wounds would soon drain his strength, he reached down and picked up his sword with his other hand and said to his men, "Follow me!" This was the last request that Isaacs asked of his command.

Cabell's brigade consisted of the 21st, 20th, 19th, 18th Arkansas Infantry, Jones' battalion and Rapley's battalion of sharp shooters. They came up against an entire division. Rosecrans had quickly reinforced Battery Powell with Hamilton's division. In spite of the overwhelming odds, the determined Arkansas troops fought their way to the works. The 20th Arkansas Regiment was over the works together with the 21st and Jones' battalion, the latter suffering very heavy losses, but they were unable to hold the fort against Hamilton's troops that were massed against them.

Their courageous assault proved to be fruitless; suffering heavy losses the besiegers were forced to retreat by an equally determined effort by the defenders to repel the attackers. The 18th and 19th Arkansas Infantry and Rapley's battery of sharp shooters went to the right of Battery Powell and followed part of Maury's division and a portion of Green's brigade into the city.[6]

Parts of the Confederate army managed to fight their way into Corinth only to be driven back by reinforcements pouring into the heat of battle. Exhausted because of lack of water, with their ammunition depleted and lacking sufficient numbers to continue their struggle, those units that managed to reach the streets of Corinth were cut off from the main body of the Confederate army and were obligated to surrender. It was obvious to all that the battle was over. In 20 minutes on that hot October day 15 officers of the 18th were killed and 105 men wounded, leaving very few able-bodied men to fight. Maury's division went into battle that morning with 3,900 men; of this number 2,500 men were lost out of the division and another 600 melted away during the retreat to Davis Bridge.

Dead at Battery Robinett After the Siege

With no other choice, the armies of Price and Van Dorn retreated south of Corinth to regroup and inventory the damage inflicted upon their armies. Captain Thrasher was captured in front of the breastworks along with a member of his company, William Ross, 25 yards from the works. They were unable to make it over the works because of the tremendous fire they were receiving that had greatly reduced their numbers. Thrasher took refuge behind a tree, and Ross got behind a log. From his position behind the log, Ross began to fire at the Yankees and killed an officer before they were both captured. Thrasher wrote, "We were held in Corinth six days. This last charge was made Saturday morning. On Monday I got permission to visit the battlefield in front of the breastworks. A detail of Federals was burying the Confederate dead. I found Ad Barbee, Bob Wilcox, and John Ross, brother of William, among the slain. I found also our colonel, John L. Daly, who commanded the 18th Arkansas, and a number of others of the regiment. It was horrible to contemplate the scene and look upon the blackened and bloated corpses."[7]

CHAPTER 8

The Battle of Davis Bridge

Van Dorn's beleaguered and tired troops were retreating west toward Pocahontas, Tennessee. They were retracing the route they had taken on the advance north into Tennessee on a poorly planned attempt to surprise Rosecrans at Corinth. The Southern army would have to find a place to cross the Tuscumsia and Hatchie Rivers soon and then turn south at Davis Bridge for the 26 mile march to Ripley. Van Dorn had placed General Lovell's division in the rear of his command. He was hoping Lovell's fresh troops could delay General McPherson's pursuit. Lovell's division sustained the least casualties at Corinth, and Van Dorn hoped he could stop the Yankees. General Maury's division had the greatest percentage of loss and was placed in the front of the retreat. Even though Maury had suffered greatly and was depleted of some of his best fighting men and officers, part of his command would be called upon to save the day at Davis Bridge.

Van Dorn's reconnaissance made him aware that another Union army from Bolivar, Tennessee, would be pressing him hard and was fast closing on his army at the Hatchie River. It was a matter of time before Major General Stephen Hurlbut with 5,000 fresh troops, who were descending down from Bolivar, Tennessee, would soon attack. To add to his dilemma Rosecrans was mounting a pursuit and would be soon nipping at Van Dorn's tucked tail. The prospects of fighting fresh troops troubled Van Dorn. He would have to find a suitable place to cross the river rapidly. The worried Van Dorn needed a commander with a cool head to take a stand. Several of his officers were disgusted with him and were questioning his leadership, he knew, and they would blame the disastrous defeat at Corinth on him. He knew that he could trust Maury and called upon his bloodied division to hold off the pursuing Union armies until Van Dorn could escape across the Hatchie River.[1],[2]

Cabell's shot-up brigade had been reduced to 550 men; a great number of his command had been left dead in the field, wounded or captured, during the assault on Battery Powell. After leaving Corinth, his battle-weary troops stopped for the night and bivouacked on the south side of the Memphis and Charleston Railroad at Chewalla, Tennessee, on the night of October

4. The next morning Cabell was assigned to the rear of the Southern army and would be called upon to fight a desperate battle against overwhelming odds. Cabell writes, "I only numbered all told, on the morning 5th, previous to marching to Davis Bridge, across the Hatchie River, 550 men. Mine was the rear brigade in the division, and owing to the order of march that day, some distance in rear of the advance brigade, which became engaged with a greatly superior force of the enemy immediately after crossing the Hatchie River. When the cannonading in front was first heard, I was then crossing the Tuscumbia River, a distance of five miles. I received an order from General Maury while crossing the river to move rapidly to the front to support of General Moore."[3]

Moore's brigade and Captain Dawson's artillery were ordered to occupy the Metamora Ridge on the east bank of the Hatchie River in order to delay the pursuit. Moore's brigade formed battle lines on the ridge, but could not hold the ridge because of overwhelming numbers of Federal troops who drove him from positions and disabled his artillery. Most of Moore's men were taken prisoners and were forced to take cover along the river's edge. W. A. Lee, a member of the 15th Arkansas Infantry, Moore's brigade, wrote, "We lay down until their fire slackened a little, and then we made good use of time to get back to the river. We bore downstream a little and chanced to find a tall sycamore that had fallen squarely across the river near the other bank with drift in the top that helped us to get to its trunk. It made a very good footbridge, and all got away that made a strong effort; so their trap slipped. I do not know how many men we lost out of our brigade. I suppose our loss was heaviest on the left side of the brigade near the bridge."[4]

Cabell's troops were called upon to reinforce the ridge, and they took up positions to the left of General Phifer's brigade. The 18th Arkansas Infantry would see action during this courageous stand by Cabell's depleted brigade on the heights.[5] Maury's division would hold off a Union army four times his number for six and one-half grueling hours without relief. The casualties Maury inflicted on the numerically superior Union army numbered 570 men during the courageous stand at Davis Bridge.[6] Cabell's brigade ran out of ammunition and with nothing left but fixed bayonets were prepared to stand and hold their ground. Realizing this, Maury ordered Cabell to retreat in good order, but the Union army had already lost heart and was making preparations to withdraw from the field. This was truly one of the darkest moments during the Civil War, because if Cabell's brigade had lost its position on the ridge, it probably would have meant that Van Dorn's entire army would have been destroyed. Incredible as it may seem, when Cabell withdrew, his losses were light, two killed and eight wounded, considering the length of time they had to hold the ridge. Tom Martin, who was a member of Company G, 18th Arkansas Infantry, wrote an article in the <u>Confederate Veteran Magazine</u> in 1909 on the retreat south to Ripley, stating that the 18th escaped across the Hatchie River at Lumpkins Mill. Quoting from another letter written by J. N. Parker, who was a member of Company I, 18th Arkansas Infantry, "We fought the Battle of Davis Mill on the Hatchie River, after the battle went to Holly Springs under General Pendleton and from there To Port Hudson, Louisiana."[7] It would be interesting to note that the 18th Arkansas was referred to as the Bloody 18th during their service at Port Hudson.[8]

There is no way of fully determining the nature of Isaacs' wounds, but it can be safe to say that again the weather played a major role in his fate. A soldier wounded during the cold winter months had a much better chance of survival than one wounded in the heat of summer or fall. A wound near a vital organ, such as the intestines, was a sure death sentence. This type of injury increased the possibility of infection, which was often fatal.

During the retreat south, Isaacs was moved south with the army, possibly to Camp Tiphan or a field hospital near there. Again, Cabell's official report points to this location. On October 10, 1862, George Isaacs died in the presence of his friends and those who labored with him in a hopeless effort to secure their freedom from Yankee interference. This conflict would continue for more than two years, and history would testify to the tragedy of it.

A young Southern lady who was living at Ripley when Van Dorn and his staff arrived there wrote a letter about the retreat. Van Dorn told her father that he would not make a stand at Ripley, and there would be little danger of fight in the immediate vicinity. Van Dorn didn't have time to linger there because McPherson was not too far behind him. The same lady wrote, "The Yankees got in town about midnight, close on the heels of our retreating army: in fact, but three or four hours behind them."[9] She helped take care of the wounded, and many were left at Ripley because of the severity of their wounds; they couldn't be moved any farther. I do not believe that Isaacs was one of the wounded left in the care of the town's people at Ripley, but was moved farther west near Holly Springs

Cabell wrote a report dated October 10, 1862, from Camp Tippah, Mississippi, then the headquarters of Maury's division, about the Battle of Corinth and the pursuit of the Confederate forces to Ripley. His report could possibly reveal the location of where Isaacs died October 10, 1862. Another possibility could be Lumpkins Mill located 6 miles south of Holly Springs where the 18th was camped at the time they were ordered to report to Port Hudson.

The Tippah River is about 10 miles east of Holly Springs and would be a good location to defend the eastern approaches to the town. Van Dorn had retreated to Holly Springs with the Army of West Tennessee and set up his headquarters there. It is evident that Isaacs was severely wounded, but not killed, on October 4, 1862, during the ferocious fighting that took place in Corinth. Sergeant Richard T. Stockton, as well as other members of his company, must have assisted him as they withdrew from the battlefield. It must have been hard on him, moving over wagon roads full of ruts created by the movement of large numbers of troops during the evacuation.[10]

His obituary appeared in the True Democrat, March 4, 1863:

"Died near Corinth, Miss., October 10, 1862, Lieut. George W. Isaacs aged 23 years. Prior to our national difficulties, he had just finished a classical education, and had commenced the study of law, with brilliant prospects for the future, but as one of the sons of Arkansas, he responded at an early day to his country's call. He received a severe wound from a grape shot at the battle of Oak Hills, but so soon as he had partially recovered; he raised a company and rushed again to his country's rescue. In a charge on the Federal fortifications at Corinth, on the 4th of Oct., he received a wound in the right hand, three of his fingers were shot off and his sword knocked out of his hand; he picked it up with his left hand and rushed on in the charge, when terminated his mortal existence on the 10th. Amidst his severe sufferings he was not heard to utter one word of complaint and died as the truly brave alone can die. He was a member of the Methodist E. Church, and we trust that he's gone to the land where shall be no more wars, sickness, pain and death. To his aged parent, I would say, weep not for your devoted son, he will not be forgotten, and when the night of death is past you will see him again in that Heaven, 'where friends shall meet again who have loved,' and shall part no more."[11]

Isaacs' death must have been exceptionally difficult for Silas and Sarah to accept. Silas was 60 years old and Sarah 52 years old at the time of his death. At any age it's hard to lose a child, and it can be especially hard on the emotions of an older person who is under constant worry, stress, and anxiety born of war.

CHAPTER 9

Port Hudson: A Confederate Fortress on the Mississippi

Port Hudson; Defenses Overlooking the Mississippi

Special Orders Number One was issued by Brigadier General John S. Bowen's division camped near Lumpkins Mill, Mississippi, on October 21, 1862. The order dealt with transporting several regiments by rail, including the 14th, 17th, 16th, 18th Infantry, Adams, and Jones Arkansas Infantry. The order reads, "The following details of troops will be made from this division to report as soon as practicable at the Waterford Station, on the railroad. They will be provided with three days' cooked rations: will take all their baggage, tents with them."[1] Waterford Station is located a few miles south of Holly Springs and not too far from Lumpkins Mill where the 18th was camped. The Confederates were using the railroad station as a staging ground to transport troops south into Louisiana.

Lumpkins Mill is approximately 350 miles from Port Hudson, and this is a long distance to march battle-weary troops who were needed in Louisiana. Fortunately for the 18th, the Mississippi Central Railroad was still in Confederate hands and the rail ride south would give them a brief rest before being assigned to the garrison duty at Port Hudson.

The Mississippi Central Railroad runs south from Holly Springs, passing through Osyka and Tangipahoa, Mississippi, located northeast of Port Hudson and then running south on to New Orleans. R. T. Martin of Company G, 18th Arkansas wrote that they were sent to Jackson by rail and from there traveled to Tangipahoa. Tangipahoa is a stop on the Mississippi Central Railroad, and after getting off the train they marched overland to Clinton.[2] They could have made the remainder of the trip on the Clinton and Port Hudson Railroad because the Confederates were using the rail line to move heavy cannons and supplies to the fort. It took them seven or eight days to arrive at their new assignment on November 1, 1862, and rail transportation offers the best possibility to explain how they got there.[3]

The casualty rate suffered by Cabell's brigade at Corinth was horrendous, and because of this only remnants of the depleted 18th Arkansas Infantry left Lumpkins Mill and marched into Port Hudson, Louisiana, after being transported by rail.[4] The Official Records list the casualty rate of the 18th Arkansas as 128 men killed, wounded, or missing during the battle.[5]

General William Nelson Rector Beall, commanding officer at Port Hudson, wanted a rapid buildup of troops to strengthen that garrison at the fort. He called for reinforcements on October 22, 1862. General Pemberton, responding to Beall's petition, issued orders putting troops into motion and by doing so strengthened the garrison from the impending attack. Pemberton was aware of the Union buildup that was under way. On December 14, 1862, Major General Nathaniel P. Banks arrived in New Orleans to take command of the Department of Mississippi from General Butler. On his arrival Banks began amassing supplies and men for an attack against the Confederate stronghold, and it continued to grow under his command.[6] To add to the Confederate high command concerns, Rear Admiral Farragut was assembling a powerful fleet of war steamers and ironclads especially designed to deliver barrages of deadly accurate rifled cannon fire. He hoped to run the gauntlet of Confederate batteries and cut off supplies being shipped on the Red River.

Farragut was no stranger to fronting heavy guns manned by skillful gunners determined to sink his fleet into a watery grave. He had proven at Fort Jackson and St. Philip the possibility of rushing past fixed positions that were filling the air with a fiery barrage of projectile mailed to his ships. It was this fronting of these batteries protecting New Orleans that led to the surrender of the city and the opening of the Mississippi to the Federal fleet. Farragut was a resourceful, determined commander and was eager to duplicate the same success at Port Hudson.

Port Hudson was of critical importance to the Confederate defense of the Mississippi. The fortifications built there by the Confederate army were strategically located on high bluffs overlooking a sharp bend in the river. The bluffs are located on the east side of the Mississippi and are elevated 85 feet above the river at the highest point. Any Union naval gunboat was in clear view and had to slow down when making a turn at this point in the river. Because of its ideal location Confederate gunners could easily defend it. To add to the strategic significance, Baton Rouge was located a short 20 miles below the Confederate garrison.

Perhaps no other place on the Mississippi River gave the Confederates a more formidable position to defend Southern commerce then Port Hudson. The fortress of Port Hudson was designed to complement the heavily fortified stronghold of Vicksburg, 110 miles upriver from Port Hudson. Forty miles above Port Hudson lay the mouth of the Red River. The Red River heavily factored into Southern strategy because it was her main artery connecting the Confederacy to the resources of Texas. Destined for the eastern theater, large quantities of grain and cattle flowed down the river to the armies of General Lee. Union strategists were equally aware of the importance of the conquest and occupation of the Red River Valley. General Nathaniel Banks had left New York with 20,000 men and on arrival at New Orleans combined his army with 10,000 troops that were stationed there.[7] Banks' success in achieving his goals would be measured by how quickly his invasion forces were able to overwhelm the small garrison assigned to Port Hudson.

All the ingredients were now in place, and the stage was set for the longest siege in United States military history, which would last 48 days. Even though Farragut had proven himself by the opening of the Mississippi River, the determined, courageous resistance by a relatively small Confederate garrison against overwhelming odds would frustrate his efforts to promptly execute his further success.

Banks' military career would suffer, and history would not favorably record the tactics he employed to secure this small piece of real estate on the Mississippi. Banks amassed nearly 40,000 Federals, which were opposed by a garrison of fewer than 7,000 Confederates. They were able to keep the

Union army at bay for nearly two months, during spring and early summer of 1863. The attempt to take the fortifications proved to be a slaughter for the Union, and this would haunt Banks throughout his career.

Sergeant Richard T. Stockton appears on the muster role of Company H, 18th Arkansas Infantry from August 31, 1862, to December 31, 1862. This would indicate that he arrived with the 18th in November. The company muster role also lists him as enlisting from January to July of 1863 for periods of three months, but also states that he was absent on detailed duty as a carpenter At Port Hudson. He is listed on the muster roll as a mechanic assigned to the Arkansas 18th Infantry, Company H. While stationed at Priceville, Mississippi, he was assigned to Maury's division, Army of the West.[8] It is interesting to note, because Stockton must have been busy, along with other mechanics, repairing gun carriages, rebuilding damaged bunkers, and replacing equipment vital to the survival of the garrison throughout the siege. It is more than probable that a lot of the work was assigned to the engineers and done under fire; Federal artillery had no respect for carpenters, especially if they wore gray coats.

On December 27, 1862, Major General Franklin Garner took command of the fort and brought with him orders to further strengthen the fortifications and make her defenses impregnable. Garner was born in New York on January 29, 1823, and graduated from the U.S. Military Academy at West Point in 1843. Before the war, he had served on frontier duty in Texas and Louisiana. His earlier presence in the area had given him knowledge of its people, which must have been a factor in his determination to hold on so long against overwhelming odds.[9],[10]

Garner had previous experience in engineering and put his knowledge to work correcting weaknesses he found in the defenses that had been put into place before his arrival. He implemented a plan to redesign the river defenses and combined the larger caliber guns, which enabled his batteries to support each other with a heavier concentration of field fire. Lacking qualified engineers, Garner drew from his command men who had some experience in construction and in supervising men.[11]

R. T. Martin, a private in the 18th Arkansas Infantry, Company G, wrote, "We were put to work building breastworks, which we completed for five miles around the fort at a point on the north side, which remained unfinished until after the siege opened on us by General Banks' army."[12]

Stockton was stationed at Port Hudson from January to February 1863, during this period when Gardner strengthened the defenses at Port Hudson. The drawing out of every available man that had some knowledge of construction from Gardner's command could account for the remarks on his records, listing him absent on detailed duty as a carpenter. Stockton and others with similar experience would be called upon to accomplish the work that Gardner hoped for, which was to make the fortress impregnable. This would not be an easy task, for Farragut's fleet would have an edge; mounting heavy naval guns, they could easily obliterate any well-planned defenses.

Private Granville McGuire, like other soldiers, had duel responsibilities keeping him busy while stationed there. Besides preparations to strengthen the earthen works that protected the fort, they were still required to drill regularly. Being confined to the post with nothing more to do than repetitive, routine duties that were required must have been monotonous to some of the men. In order to break their boredom some of the men made beer from corn and molasses that were in good supply from the commissary. This concoction didn't sound like it would be worth advertising, but its fame grew as a somewhat agreeable drink, and a thriving enterprise developed in trading Port Hudson's unique brew. Rev. J. H. M'Neilly was stationed at Port Hudson and wrote an article for the <u>Confederate Veteran Magazine</u>. He wrote, "Another delicacy which found ready sale was made of flour and mashed sweet potatoes baked into a round cake and called sweet potato pone. Several of our regiments were so pushing in this industry, peddling pones through the camp, that the 30th Louisiana, a French-speaking regiment, would call out as they went out to drill; 'Here comes your sweet tater the pones.'"[13]

Because molasses was not in short supply and could easily be made into candy, the men wasted no time in making molasses candy to satisfy their sweet tooth. Groups of men composed of two made up the fort candy brigade. They could be seen in different parts of the post pulling on ropes of amber-like taffy until it reached the right consistency and became brittle. These enterprises developed a unique way of gaining a better grip on the sticky stuff by spitting on their hands. In spite of these unsanitary conditions, these were the days before we had government inspectors, other groups of men eagerly awaited the finished product.

Large plantations located near Port Hudson supplied the garrison with sweet potatoes, pumpkins, and flour available in good supply for baking bread before the siege. Good beef was not available. M'Neilly wrote, "The memory of the beef that was served to us for a good while is still nauseating. Poor, gristly blue, gummy, it could be boiled for hours and never an eye of grease on the water. Those old steers, I suppose, were the only animals in existence without a single particle of fat in their composition."[14]

A boatload of fresh pork arrived at Port Hudson sometime during the winter and brought back memories of "hog killing time." Most of the country boys, I'm sure, had memories of how they looked forward to butchering hogs fattened for this purpose. Hog killing was a big event in rural life because it ensured the survival of the family throughout the harsh winter months. The meat was easily preserved and could be stored in smokehouses for future use.

Their dreams of sausage and spareribs, "things that where," had come true, and the manifestations of these fantasies became more than their stomachs could handle. The memory of Mother standing before an open fireplace early in the morning preparing the first meal before daylight, the aroma of fresh-cooked sausage and perhaps biscuits and gravy made from lard must have been overwhelming. Soon their mess and stomachs were filled with these spicy delicacies, and before the next morning the results of "pigging out" were apparent, for the services of the camp doctors were urgently requested. The boys gradually adjusted to "Mom's" home cooking. Gardens of vegetables were cultivated during the spring that added more variety to their diet. Planting gardens must have been therapeutic, for I'm sure it helped to relieve their constant homesickness as well as to improve their health.

Fortunately for Stockton and McGuire, the unusually cold weather broke early in the Gulf States. The region was experiencing some of the coldest temperatures in 25 years. It is normally warm in southern Louisiana during the winter months. Port Hudson is located approximately 150 miles north of the Gulf, and the coastal plains are typically mild. A soldier stationed at the fort in a letter back home writes, "It is very warm down here the peach trees is in bloom." The following letter was written during the latter part of February. Perhaps the weather was conditioning the officers for an ordeal that was yet to come. After the surrender of the garrison, the officers were shipped to Johnson Island, a barren piece of real estate located off the shore of Lake Erie. This area even today is referred to as a deep freeze, for it is not unusual for the region to receive four feet of snow at a time. They were experiencing a cold winter, and weather broke in February in Louisiana. The harsh, bitter, unforgiving cold they would experience as prisoners on Johnson Island would remind them of the forgiving southern winter of 1863 at Port Hudson.[15]

Port Hudson, Louisiana, February the 25th 1863

"Dear father and mother, I seat myself to write you a few lines to let you know that I am tolerable well and I hope these few lines may come safe to hand and find you all well. I sent forty dollars to you by Tom Page and he furnished to leave it at Doctor Issacks, and I want to buy anything you want with it and I will send you some more as soon as I get the chance. I want you to write whether they have burned up all of the cotton about there or not.

Tell Ransom to stay at home as long as he can and not to go to war until he gets old enough. It is very warm down here the peach trees is bloom out. I drew 169 dollars. It is reported they are fighting at Vicksburg, Mississippi. It is reported that General Banks is advancing on this place. Though I don't no how many men he has. So I must close right soon and give me all the news and excuse my short letter and bad writing and I will try to do better next time."[16]

The writer of the letter has written to his parents, who were living in Saline County, Arkansas, during the siege. He describes his lot there at the post as being tolerable, and doesn't seem to be overly excited about Banks' impending buildup of Union forces. Perhaps what he is reflecting is the monotonous routine most soldiers had to go through each day. Reveille was at daybreak, and if it were a clear day the morning sun casting her first rays upon the muddy Mississippi would greet him. They would then line up in formation for roll call and present arms for inspection, then police the grounds. The soldiers' day was filled with routine drills that would reoccur throughout the day. Some of the regiments included a dress parade as a final act of discipline, and then the troopers could look forward to a friendly, beckoning good-bye as the setting sun's rays reflected against their poorly constructed, shabby barracks.

By early March, winter's dreary scenery lay behind them, and nature was busy ushering in a new landscape with trees laden with green buds bursting, wild flowers dancing in a warm breeze and all the renewal that spring brings that farm families hope for. W. C. Porter, a member of the 16th Arkansas Infantry, was enjoying the good weather and dreaming about being back home in Arkansas for planting time. He wrote in his diary dated March 5, 1863, that it was, "Nice corn planting weather but I fear that I will not plant any this year."

It was approaching the middle of March, and the weather was still warm. The evenings had been uneventful, and the garrison was becoming used to the sounds of the night that were announcing spring was approaching. Most of the men were sons of pioneer families, and they had grown accustomed to the familiar voices of the evening. They could hear the whippoorwill's whistle in the near distance with its repetitive serenade that only one who grew up on the frontier could appreciate. Soon the crickets would add their "chirp," and the bullfrogs would chime in "jug of rum," while other frogs would add "nee deep" to nature's symphony. The garrison had bivouacked, wrapped in the reassuring comfort and serenity of nature's chorus.

On March 14 the peaceful nights they had been experiencing would end and be replaced by exploding shells and manmade thunder that could be heard in Baton Rouge 20 miles away. Farragut would attempt to deliver a cargo of destruction from his powerful fleet of warships and mortar boats at night. All preparations had been made by Farragut to store aboard his ships munitions that were designed to leave little traces of the Confederate batteries. He was confident that he would not be delayed and that he could eliminate any threat to his fleet by the use of his superior firepower. It was his hope that by quickly passing the defenses of Port Hudson he would be able to write another chapter in a series of successes.

Admiral Farragut's Flagship

His powerful fleet had been anchored below the fort and was awaiting orders to weigh anchor. Even though the defenders were outgunned, nature would play a decisive role in determining the outcome of any attempt to pass the fortified bluffs.[17] Farragut would have to contend with bluffs soaring above the river 80 feet or more that would add to his difficulties in a successful passage of the river batteries. The Confederates had ideally positioned their heavy guns on the heights, which gave them an advantage, even though most of their guns were outdated. The Union fleet would have to pass through treacherous waters; the opposite shore was plagued by numerous eddies that would force his ships to navigate the narrow channel on the eastern bank directly under the Confederate batteries. The challenge to his powerful squadron would be further intensified by a swift five knot current that would reduce his progress to a snail's pace directly under the mouth of Southern cannon manned by skillfully trained gunners under the command of Lieutenant Colonel Paul Francis De Gournay. De Gournay had earned his reputation during Lee's campaigns along Peninsula in Virginia.

At 2 p.m. Farragut ordered his mortar boats to open fire on the garrison with a barrage from his immense 13-inch sea mortars. Each mortar could fire a 220-pound bomb up to 4,325 yards, which made them impregnable, because the Confederate artillery was unable to match this range. Because of their capabilities Farragut was hoping to use these weapons to soften the Confederate defenses. The first incoming missiles alerted the garrison to the impending attack. The long roll sounded, calling the men to form ranks and fall in.[18]

J. M. M'Neilly wrote, "It was well after dark when the enemy's vessels silently got underway, but the movement was discovered almost immediately. The big fires were lighted, and the river for miles was as a bright day. The long roll sounded, and the infantry were marched to the breastworks back from the river; we supposed that General Banks would make a land attack from his post at Baton Rouge.

"Then was seen the grandest display, the activity of death's enginery. The roar of the guns, the explosion of the shells, some of them high in the air, the shrill of the steam whistles, the glare of the great bon fires, all combine to make a sublime spectacle. Very soon we realized that the enemy's shot were going over us and doing no damage, while on the other hand our shots were telling."[19]

By 9 p.m. the order was given to weigh anchor and the squadron was signaled to launch the attack. It took until 10 p.m. to combine and coordinate the attack by the entire fleet. The Hartford was Farragut's flagship, and she would be the first to test the Rebel batteries. The Hartford was built at the Boston Naval Yard and launched in November 1858. She was 225 feet long and displaced 2,900 tons, drawing 17 feet. The Hartford mounted 20 nine-inch Dahlgren guns, two 20-pound parrot rifles and two 12-pounders. The guns were designed by John Dahlgren of the U.S. Navy to fire shells against wooden ships.

The Albatross was lashed to Hartford's side, giving her twin-screw capacity, increasing maneuverability against a strong five knot current, which they would have to push against in the passing. By lashing the two ships together Farragut felt it would increase the odds for success. This was done because if one ship was disabled, the other had the capacity to continue up river and sail out of range. Farragut had tied himself to the rigging; he did not want to be thrown overboard by the impact of incoming shells during the battle.[20],[21] This was the same admiral who would enter Mobile Bay later in the war and issue the order, "Damn the torpedoes! Full speed ahead!"

Following behind Farragut's flagship came Richmond, with the Genesee lashed to her side. Behind her steamed the Monongahela with the Kineo lashed to her side. Next following in this procession sailed the Mississippi unassisted, steaming on her own power.[22],[23]

Before the bombardment began, Lieutenant Colonel J. E. Smith, commanding officer in charge of heavy artillery, had inspected the batteries to make sure they were ready and that the necessary munitions were in place.

The Confederate high command was on alert because of the unusually high concentration of warships that were anchored near Profit Island, three miles below the fortifications. Garner's Signal Corps under the command of Captain J. M. Youngblood was positioned on the east bank of the Mississippi, opposite Troth's Landing and was on alert ready to report any movement of the Union fleet.[24] Other precautions had been made to ensure that Farragut's fleet would not pass undetected at night. Piles of lighter pine, pine that had decomposed, leaving pieces with high concentrations of resin that would readily ignite even in damp weather, were waiting to be ignited. These fires were designed to illuminate the river and prevent Farragut from passing undetected, cloaked in darkness.[25]

By 11 p.m. the Hartford had moved close enough to be in range of De Gournay's guns. A lookout had sighted the Hartford and had fired a rocket, alerting his battery that she was approaching. Soon an eight-inch shell was fired, but the gunners aimed too high, and the missile exploded over the Albatross, causing no damage.

Farragut was strapped to the ship's rigging, reinforcing the tradition that would climax in Mobile Bay when he would give the order, "Damn the torpedoes! Full speed ahead!"[26] His teenage son, Loyall, was aboard the Hartford as a non-combatant. Fleet Surgeon J. M. Foltz urged the admiral to allow Loyall to assist him in a safer area of the ship where he would be protected from incoming shells. The admiral insisted that the boy remain on deck; replying to Foltz he said, "No, that will not do. It is true our only child is on board by chance, and he is not in the service; but, being here, he will act as one of my aides, to assist in conveying my orders during the battle, and we will trust in Providence...." Perhaps Providence was about to shine down favorably upon the older admiral and his young son, because when the Hartford approached the lower batteries, a shot whistled by Loyall, and he ducked down, attempting to evade the projectile. On seeing his son's reaction, the admiral grabbed his shoulders and yelled above what must have been the deafening roar of discharging cannons, "Don't duck, my son, there is no use in trying to dodge God Almighty."[27]

Lieutenant Colonel Smith, who had served under Farragut before the war, was waiting patiently at Battery 4 to welcome his old commander with a greeting that was far from polite. The Hartford passed Battery 4, hugging the east bank of the river so close to the river's edge that the officers were easy targets for marksmen with a rifle or pistol. Smith's heart must have been pounding at the site of the old man presenting himself as such an easy target. A pistol shot from cannoneers was not a worthy challenge to the older admiral who was boldly defying the odds. "Instead, he double loaded an 8-inch and 10-inch columbiad to pay respects to his former commander; he

62

personally trained the 10-inch on the <u>Hartford</u>, but when he gave the order to fire, both friction primers failed. Replacing them, again Smith gave the order to fire. Once more, both primers misfired, and the <u>Hartford</u> passed unstitched."[28]

For everything there is a season and a time for every matter under heaven, according to the writer of Ecclesiastics. These reoccurring close calls with death during the battle seemed to confirm the admiral's belief. As the battle continued it became obvious that it wasn't his time. The discharge from the fleet's cannons combined with smoke from the fires had created a smoke screen and it became difficult to distinguish between friend and foe. The poor visibility made it increasingly hard for the pilot to navigate the hazardous five-knot current.

The sound of the ship running aground must have signaled to the crew that Providence's good fortunes had come to an end, for they were directly under the mouth of Southern cannons. Johnny Reb, seizing upon the opportunity to capture the prize, began to fire rounds of musket fire into the <u>Hartford</u>. I think it would be safe to assume the cannoneers were confident they would settle the score and finish the job the riflemen started. They lowered their artillery, but they were unable to do any damage to the ship because they could not lower their cannon far enough to hit it. The <u>Albatross</u> lashed to the side of <u>Hartford</u> strained as she reversed engines while <u>Hartford</u> pushed forward. This maneuver freed the ships, and both continued to steam up the river out of range of Confederate guns.

To paraphrase Paul Harvey, that's not the end of the story. The <u>Hartford's</u> sister ship the <u>Richmond</u> was moving up somewhere behind her. The captain aboard the <u>Richmond</u> could see flashes of cannon fire. Believing this was enemy fire, he ordered the <u>Richmond</u> to make ready for a broadside. Just before he was ready to issue the order the smoke cleared, and the crew of <u>Richmond</u> realized they were about to sink the <u>Hartford</u>. Surely by now Loyall Farragut must have believed his father's words.[29],[30]

Next to test the accuracy of the Rebel batteries steamed the <u>Richmond</u> with the <u>Genesee</u> lashed to her side, both comforted by one another, hoping the two could prevail as one against the treacherous waters that lay ahead. Soon the air was filled with screams from a crewman aboard the flagship <u>Hartford</u> who had fallen overboard. Responding quickly to the man's cries of desperation, Lieutenant Edward Terry without hesitation yelled to the crew of the <u>Richmond</u>, "Man overboard. Throw him a rope." A rope was quickly thrown in the direction of the sound of the stricken man crying for help and a splash could be heard as the rope uncoiled, landing in the water. The sound of the splash was soon followed by an eerie silence that clearly witnessed that the muddy waters of the Mississippi had swallowed their victim into a watery grave.

Their confidence shaken by this bad omen, the Richmond steamed into clouds of smoke created by the fires the Confederates had lit on the riverbanks, with discharging cannon intensifying the blanket. Surrounded and enveloped by these noxious fumes only reinforced the uncertainty of what lay ahead, because visibility was quickly reduced to near zero. In the distance flashes of cannon fire could be seen as cannoneers on both sides attempted to deliver their deadly cargos on phantom targets, for the thick smoke was cloaking both sides.

Patiently, the Confederate gunners waited for a breeze to clear the atmosphere that would give them a chance to prove their accuracy and redeem themselves as artillerymen. They were prepared not to make the same mistakes they had made with the Hartford by letting her pass only with rifle fire that had just annoyed her.

Halfway through the obstacle course the smoke began to drift, revealing the clear silhouette of the ship's outline and giving the rebel gunners the opportunity to prove that old cannon were deadly at point-blank range, for the Richmond had unknowingly positioned itself directly under enemy guns.

Smith had failed to sink the admiral's flagship because of faulty friction primers, but this mistake would not be repeated on the Richmond. The Confederates hurried their artillery pieces to the edge of the bluff, and showing no mercy they began to pour grape and canister shot into the ship. Shells began to rip into the ship, their impacts causing the ship to repeatedly reel and shake throughout by the deadly bombardment. A solid shot had found its mark, shattering the starboard safety valve chamber and causing damage to the port safety valve.[31] The ruptured valves began to release steam, evaporating any chance of duplicating Farragut's successful passage of the batteries. The wounded and bloody ship had no choice but to turn back because of the murderous fire from the vengeful Southern guns.

Next to challenge the Confederate batteries steamed the Monongahela with Kineo lashed to her side. They were about to face veteran gunners who had learned to zero in their guns. Soon after the Kineo passed the first battery, the Confederates on the western side of the river began to fire upon the ship with rounds of musket fire. The Kineo responded with shrapnel and grapeshot, silencing the sharp shooters. The two continued to steam up the river, but a 32-pound shot had disabled the Kineo's rudder, hindering its progress. After an inspection of the damage the two ships continued in their attempt to run the gauntlet of Rebel fire, only to run aground in the worst possible place, opposite the Confederate's heaviest guns.

The impact from the collision with the shoal tore loose the gunboat <u>Kineo</u>, separating her from the larger <u>Monongahela</u>. Her freedom was but brief for she ran aground, but she managed to dislodge herself by reversing the engines and backing off the shoal. The <u>Monongahela</u> was not so fortunate, for she remained stranded on the sandbar for 25 minutes. I think it would be safe to assume that some of the Southern cannoneers were saying surely Providence has delivered our enemy into our hands. Zeroing their guns in on the helpless prey, they began to pour round after round of shot into the stranded vessel, destroying her bridge and disabling part of her guns. The smaller ship managed to help tow the larger vessel, and with the <u>Monongahela's</u> engines straining in reverse, it finally came free. Unassisted and steaming on her own power, the damaged <u>Monongahela</u> attempted again to run the batteries, but the crank pin became overheated, forcing her engines to shut down. Helpless and at the mercy of the river current, she drifted down river and out of range of the guns.

Farragut had placed the <u>Mississippi</u> last in line because he reasoned that she had the least possible chance of passing the batteries. By positioning her last she would not hinder the progress of the other ships if she became disabled.[32]

The <u>Mississippi</u> passed the lower batteries without incident, but as she approached the turn in the river her pilot miscalculated the angle of the turn and increased speed, causing the ship to run aground, anchoring the <u>Mississippi</u> to a shoal. This positioned her in a very precarious position because she was in range of Confederate artillery and unable to back off the shoal. Captain Smith ordered the engines reversed, hoping to free her, but this maneuver failed to free the ship; the <u>Mississippi</u> was stuck fast.

The Confederate gunners from three batteries zeroed their pieces in on the helpless ship, pouring shot and shell into her. Stuck fast on the sandbar, the <u>Mississippi</u> became a sitting duck. The crew of the <u>Mississippi</u> struggled for over half an hour, trying to back the ship off the sandbar. Realizing that their situation was hopeless, Smith ordered the ship to be set on fire, fearing it would fall into Rebel hands. The <u>Mississippi</u> was caught in a rain of murderous cross fire that was cutting through the ship. The Rebel gunners chose hot shot to write her obituary with, and soon the forward storeroom was ignited. The fires started by the hot shot were threatening the ship's magazines, and the captain ordered the ship to be abandoned. The <u>Mississippi</u> was stuck fast on the shoal until about 3 a.m. when it finally floated off the shoal and drifted down the river in flames.[33]

A chaplain at Port Hudson wrote, "Meanwhile the <u>Mississippi</u>, a big seventeen-gun side-wheeler, grounded opposite our hot shot batteries and was set on fire by our shot. It was a hopeless task to save her and her officers and crew got to shore as best they could." It was said, "Lieutenant Dewey jumped into the water and swam to shore. It was a magnificent site as we watched the flames rising through the rigging and reaching skyward until they came to the magazines, when a heavy explosion destroyed the vessel."[34] The writer was referring to Lieutenant George Dewey who would become famous during the Spanish American War. Admiral George Dewey would sail the American fleet into Manila Bay during the war and destroy the Spanish fleet there. It is interesting to note that other accounts have Dewey and the captain leaving last in small boats after the crew and sick were evacuated from the burning <u>Mississippi</u>.

Four days after the bombardment, Colonel William N. Parrish, who commanded the 18th Arkansas Infantry, took time to write to his wife. It is interesting to take note that the 18th was bivouacked near the breastworks and were awakened by the sounds of the first incoming shells from Farragut's fleet.

Port Hudson Louisiana
March 18, 1863

My own dear wife,
"We have gained a signal victory over the Yankees. We were attacked last night by the Federal fleet. It resulted in a heavy loss to the Yanks. Our batteries succeeded in burning one of their best seagoing frigates mounted with 22 guns and the sinking of another. Two boats succeeded in passing our batteries though it cannot do the Feds much good. As it will keep them busy to keep our Red River gunboats off of them. The scene during the engagement was the most beautiful that I have ever beheld. Though there was some terror it was interesting. The first we knew of the attack was the Yankee thunder busting from their mortar boats. We were aroused from our pleasant slumber where we were reposing in line of battle near our breastworks. Soon after the roaring the mortar boats their whole fleet was brought in to requisition (9 or 10 in number). They were soon in range of our batteries when they busted forth their destruction to the Yankees and Yankee boats, some throwing hot shot, some solid shot, and some shell.

"I cannot express the awful noise, it seemed as though the whole world was exploding and the air was filled with shot and shell (red hot shot) shells exploding in the pieces whistling in every direction, but strange to say there was but one or two of our men killed and about six or seven wounded, God is on our side. Their land forces advance within six or eight miles of this place where they were met by our men and drove back to their breastworks at Baton Rouge. The Yanks are still making demonstrations as though the fight was still to be continued. Their boats drew up in line of battle below our batteries yesterday and commenced a terrific firing, but our batteries treated them with contempt. They were too far off to do any damage. I suppose they wanted to draw our batteries to get their range but they failed. They are still lay in sight. We will not be surprised if we are attacked in 24 hours and have a general engagement. We are ready for them at any moment let them come. We will give them the best in the shop. We have reports of fighting going on at Vicksburg, however they have not sent any more gunboats past. The capture of their gunboats <u>Indianola</u> and the <u>Queen of the West</u> has give them a warning of their danger."[35]

CHAPTER 10

The Big Bushwhack

Cannon at Port Hudson State Park

The 18th was assigned to Brigadier General William N. R. Beall's brigade. He was responsible for defending the center on May 27. Colonel I. G. W. Steedman was positioned on Beall's left, Colonel W. R. Miles on Beall's right, and Colonel William B. Shelby commanded the left on Steedman's line. Beall's brigade consisted of the 49th Alabama, 8th Battalion and the 12th, 14th, 16th, 18th, and 23rd Arkansas. Detachments of the 11th and 17th Arkansas and the 1st Mississippi were assigned to his sector along with supporting batteries.

On May 27, the 18th was ordered to relieve the 1st Alabama Infantry Regiment the day the first assault began. They occupied the Alabama Arkansas redoubt and were stationed there during the offensive against the left wing of the fortifications.[1] They would hold this position during the Union onslaught on the 27th and would be called upon to reinforce other units that day. Colonel William N. Parish commanded the 18th Arkansas Infantry during the Federal advance of May 27.[2] Parrish helped organize a company of the 18th in Saline County, Arkansas, which was made up of men from Simpson and Washington Townships. His regiment along with other units would repeatedly be ordered to defend different positions along the 4.5 miles of earthen breastworks until the surrender on July 9. The Confederates were greatly outnumbered and had limited resources of manpower to defend the works that were originally designed to accommodate 20,000 men. Because of this General Gardner shifted his command around like a shell game in order to strengthen weak positions that were threatened with an impending Union attack during the siege.

The Alabama Arkansas redoubt was located to the left of Commissary Hill. Preventing the Federals from taking Commissary Hill was a top priority in Gardner's strategy to hold Port Hudson. The hill commanded a strategic location where the Confederates could fire on any Union assault from this vantage point. Behind Commissary Hill the arsenal, gristmill, and commissary stores were located.[3] Steedman's forces on the left consisted of the 10th, 15th, and 18th Arkansas, the 39th Mississippi, and the 1st Alabama Infantry along with supporting batteries on the day of the attack.

Lt. Howard Wright wrote that on the 27th, Beall reinforced Steedman's left. Steedman needed reinforcements quickly in order to meet the Union assault that morning and strengthen the threatened points on his line. The 18th Arkansas Infantry was one of the units that reinforced the left during the attack.[4] We cannot fully determine the exact location of the different regiments on the 27th because they were in constant motion, strengthening weak positions in the Confederate defenses. We can understand the pivotal points to which they were anchored during this part of the siege, but the precise movements of the troops across the Southern lines might not ever be fully determined.

The attack that morning by Banks didn't come as a surprise, for the Confederates knew it was about to happen. The previous day Banks had issued an order, "Port Hudson must be taken tomorrow."[5] His plan called for a general assault on the entire Confederate works. Heavy skirmishing had occurred on the 25th along Steedman's entire front along the closest positions held by the Union advance, with Banks attempting to inch his way as close as possible to the breastworks. The heavy artillery bombardment that morning had clearly alerted the defenders, leaving no question that Union assaulting columns would soon appear out of the woods. The defenders clearly understood that they could not match the Union's overwhelming superiority in manpower, but they would have to rely upon their determination not to relinquish their positions in the face of the intimidating numbers. It was clearly understood by both officers and enlisted men that no man would be excused from his duty, and the only accepted way to abandon his assignment would be to leave not alive.[6]

The prospects of a conflict had heightened the defenders' awareness of their surroundings. Their sharpened senses were trained upon the woods located beyond clearings that ringed the breastworks, waiting for any movement. They were ready to spring to action at the first sounds coming from the forest, signaling an attack was approaching.

The first attack began by General Godfrey Weitzel about 6 a.m. in the woods along Steedman's right and center.[7] The Yankees' advance would encounter an obstacle course of thick undergrowth, ravines choked with fallen timbers, and a forest of dense magnolia trees. Colonel Locke's 1st Alabama was waiting in the woods, taking advantage of every ravine and the numerous hills covered with dense foliage. Many of the Alabama men were sons of frontiersmen and were experts at bushwhacking an enemy. The Union forces moved forward through this abatis of fallen timber--trees cut down by the Confederates to slow the enemy's advance--in a desperate, hard-fought struggle in difficult terrain. At every ravine, gully, and hill the Confederates were waiting in ambush to hotly contest ownership of each inch of ground during the Union advance. Even though the Confederates fought hard, they were forced back to their fortifications when the Union attack threatened both flanks. The fight in the woods resulted in heavy casualties on both sides. Locke's Confederate troops would regroup behind the works, but their determined resistance in the woods cost him 40 percent of his command.

Weitzel had assembled an imposing force of 14 Federal regiments that numbered about 6,000 troops.[8] To take a fortified position with entrenched troops supported by heavy artillery requires a force of three times that number to overwhelm the defenders. The great eighteenth century Prussian military theorist Karl Von Clausewitz cautioned that an attack against an able opponent in a good position is risky business that should only be tried after careful reconnaissance ruled out all other options for dislodging the enemy. Twelve hundred Confederates were all that Garner could spare to defend his left.[9]

The 18th Arkansas became heavily engaged when Colonel Hawkes Fearing's Union brigade attacked the bullpen in force and where called upon to reinforce this position. The bullpen was located to the right of Steedman's center behind Fort Desperate, which Colonel Ben Johnson's 15th Arkansas Infantry defended. This is where cattle were slaughtered and butchered. Steedman had anticipated that if Banks tried to overwhelm the bullpen he would have to reinforce it in order to hold it. After the attack began, Colonel O. P. Lyles' 23rd, 14th, and 18th Arkansas Infantry Regiments arrived just in time to stop Fearing's advance. The 18th on arrival began to form a line of battle behind the entrenchments. The reinforcements quickly stopped Fearing's brigade, and the Yankees were compelled to withdraw below a crest where they regrouped and returned fire.

It was just six short months earlier that the 18th Arkansas had tried to storm Battery Powell, and I am sure that Sergeant Stockton and Private McGuire were thinking about how their ranks were decimated in failed attempt to make it over the Federal works at Corinth, Mississippi. The 18th paid such an awesome price in blood that day at Corinth that they earned the name, "The bloody 18th Arkansas." They were seasoned veterans who clearly understood what siege warfare was all about, and they were now entrenched, ready to even the score.

Lines of blue-coat adversaries appeared in the open in front of Johnnie Reb, coming dangerously near. Many of these men were religious and knew the commandment of God, "Thou shall not kill." They had been taught this as youths by their pastors, elders, and mothers, and it would be safe to assume that some were experiencing guilt, fear, and anger. Others were fighting to survive and protect the friendships that had formed between them during their ordeal; they were determined not to let each other down. The boys in gray aimed their pieces low, and a strange twist in human nature was about to be unleashed; the blur of blue had blended into one mass and was no longer regarded as human. General Nathaniel Bedford Forest said, "War means fightin' and fightin' means killing."

Their adversary came closer, and they understood that in order to survive they had to kill or be killed, for the bestial nature of man was provoked. Aiming their guns it was heard, "Let's give them hell, boys! Plug them plum center every time." A coolness born of resolve to survive prevailed, and gently squeezing the trigger, a storm of minie balls were sent on a mission of destruction. Quickly they reloaded, then deliberately took time to fire low so every missile found its target. The slaughter inflicted by the Southern backwoodsmen upon the Union troops in their attempt to take the bullpen would later be referred to as, "The big gigantic bush."[10]

It would be interesting to take note that the 18th, 23rd, and 15th Arkansas charged the Union works at Corinth, and both sides inflicted heavy casualties on each other. The Arkansans understood what it meant to charge a heavily fortified position and experience defeat. They knew that the determined resistance by the Union defenders at Corinth won the battle.

The numbers were right to take the place. Unfortunately for the Union, Banks had little military experience in executing a complicated military operation, simultaneously attacking on all fronts, that was essential to take Port Hudson. The inequality between the number of defenders and besiegers proves that something was wrong; the Union army was well equipped and had the numbers to overwhelm the Southern defenders by sheer force, in spite of the difficult landscape. Banks' failure to inspire his officers to carry out his plans resulted in a Union defeat.

It was afternoon; General Sherman had been waiting to attack Beall's center. He should have advanced that morning, which would have taken pressure off Wetzel's stalled advance. Sherman had reservations about Banks' plan and felt "It was worse than folly"; confusion seemed to be the order of the day. After being ordered by Banks, he reluctantly obeyed.[11]

At 2:15 p.m. Sherman gave the orders to his division commanders and began the attack across Slaughter's field. Sherman was positioned in front of Beall's brigade and had 400 yards of open field to cross. He would have to cross open ground in front of Beall's center in order to storm the Southern positions. Emerging from the cover of the trees, the 165th New York Zouave Infantry Regiment's flashy red trousers and brightly colored uniforms contrasted with the different shades of green of the woods of the open field. Quickly they formed a battle line and accelerated into a charge, believing that their smart-spirited uniforms would bolster their morale and confidence and carry them to victory. They had adopted their military tradition from the French army of Napoleon III and had earned a reputation on the battlefield as fierce and dependable fighters in spite of their bizarre appearance.[12]

Some Zouave units, feeling that their brightly colored uniforms increased the possibility of their being singled out on the battlefield, adopted the traditional blue of the Union army. This was not the case with all the Zouaves; many fought in their traditional, colorful uniforms throughout the war. These units were recognized for their devotion to discipline and duty and were some of the best-drilled fighters the Union had.

When they came out of the woods onto Slaughter's field, their conspicuous appearance made them ideal targets for Confederate gunners. Beall's artillery was loaded with spherical case and waiting to fire their deadly rounds as soon as they were within range. Spherical case consisted of a hollow projectile containing bullets. It had a programmable timer fuse and was designed to explode in mid-flight, spraying a deadly conical-shaped pattern of bullets on an advancing infantry column. This choice of projectile was highly effective in plowing through troops at distant ranges, bursting in the midst of a column and opening up large gaps in advancing troops. This was the first choice that the Confederate gunners used at 400 to 500 yards, which was the distance across Slaughter's field that the 165th New York Zouaves had to cover in order to take the breastworks. The Yankee columns took this kind of punishment, which opened up large gaps in their ranks that quickly filled with replacements.

As they came closer and lessened the distance, the Confederate gunners chose grapeshot. Grapeshot was mainly used aboard naval vessels and did not have the range that spherical case had. It was a mid-range weapon that was used during the Union charge. A standard round of grapeshot had three tiers of two-inch diameter balls separated by iron plates and held together by a central rod which connected the top to the bottom plates and was wrapped in canvas or cloth. After the grapeshot had done its deadly work, the Confederate gunners substituted canister as the choice ordinance to finish the job of slaughter on the charging Yankees. They were now within 150 yards and canister was the most commonly used weapon at this range because it acts like a giant shotgun. Canister was one of the most feared ammunition of the Civil War. A deadly round of canister consisted of a tin can packed with sawdust and as many as 76 musket balls, which when fired, created a deadly blanket of missiles at close range, disintegrating any massed infantry. The ordinances the Confederate gunners used did their work well on the Zouaves who bravely charged into this storm. Their lines wavered, and the remainder took up defensive positions behind stumps and logs, firing at any Southern boy who was foolish enough to expose himself.[13]

Beall had sent troops early in the morning to reinforce Steedman, which weakened part of his command. When Sherman's attack began, reinforcements from Mills' right were immediately sent to strengthen the center, which was coming under heavy pressure from Sherman. The 165th New York failed in their first attack, but many were still in the field behind stumps and logs, firing at the Confederates. When the second wave emerged from the woods, three regiments strong, they quickly formed in lines of battle as though they were on drill. After forming, their officers ordered them to double-quick, hoping to finish the job the Zouaves started. An obstacle course of four fences lay between the Union and the Confederates' entrenchment. Knowing that the first attack had failed reinforced the Confederate confidence to drive back another.

The gunners were waiting with their artillery pieces loaded. They had already figured out what distance to set the timer fuses in order to explode with more deadly accuracy in the enemy's ranks. As soon as the second wave was out of the woods the gunners gave the order to fire. Momentarily, all that could be heard was the deafening roar of discharging cannon. The cannoneers were positioned at their post, acting in one accord, each with a predetermined assignment and movements that had been carefully choreographed. The Confederates knew that the odds had increased because Sherman was deploying more men for the second charge.

They had drilled hard in order to complete a sequence of commands and movements between loading and firing. If the gunner crews were doing their job well, they would be able to fire a Napoleon cannon three to four times a minute. This would be absolutely essential in order to stop the wall of blue coats that would be fast closing on their positions. The discharge from the cannon and musket fire created a thick cloud that enveloped both defenders and besiegers. The enveloping cloud reduced visibility across Slaughter's field, briefly offering some protection for the cannoneers between reloads from the Zouaves sharpshooters who were trying to pick them off.

After being driven back by the Confederate fire, the Union attackers reformed at the edge of the woods for another attempt, hoping to succeed with a renewed spirit, but the circumstances had not changed. In the earlier attempt confusion had occurred at the fences that crossed the battlefield. The Southern boys braced themselves for another attack, knowing they faced an enemy that would attempt to overwhelm their defenses by sheer force of numbers. Again charging, their officers encouraged their men forward, but their will was broken by a determined adversary; the Yankees' drive fizzled out within 50 or 60 yards from first breaking out of the protection of the woods. Some of them continued to fire from behind logs, and those that did not retreat back into the woods lay until nightfall and under the cover of darkness crawled back into the woods.

After the assault on May 27, several more attempts would be made by the Federals to breach the breastworks. According to a Confederate who was there during these assaults by Banks, the Union could have easily taken the place because they didn't have enough men to defend all points on the line. He wrote, "The siege of Port Hudson was not more credible to the Confederates than it was discernible to the Federals. We had not enough men to make a good skirmish line around our four miles of works. At the time of any one of the assaults by the Federals, when the Confederates were centered at the point of attack, the thousands of Federal soldiers not engaged could have put their hands in their pockets and leisurely walked over the greater part of the ground embraced within our works."[14]

CHAPTER 11

Trying to Hold Their Ground

Dummy Cannon Used to Fool Enemy

On June 11, 1862, the 18th Arkansas was ordered to reinforce the command of Steedman. He wrote, "From all appearance the enemy are preparing for demonstration in my front, and more particularly in front of the slaughter pen. I have made all my dispositions, and am ready to use at best advantage the force at my disposal. If the attack is made at the point I most suspect, Colonel Shelby's troops will be principally engaged, assisted by the left wing of the 18th Arkansas, posted around the battery at Bennett's house." Steedman went on to write that in spite of the mud and slop, the troops' morale was good.[1]

On the morning of June 14, Banks ordered another general assault on the works. Ferocious assaults were thrown against the defenders during the 14th. The battle took a heavy toll on the Federal forces, with regimental losses by the Union constituting some of the most severe and bloodiest of the entire Civil War: 1,805 Union troops were killed, wounded, or captured during the assault. Estimated casualties on the Union side were that more than 4,000 men had fallen from the start of the hostilities in March, and would nearly double that during the bloodbath that morning. Tom Martin of Company G, 18th Arkansas Infantry described the assault.

"In June General Banks sent in a flag of truce to General Garner demanding unconditional surrender, saying that he was in position to open on us the next morning with three hundred pieces of artillery, that he was prepared to take the fort, and that as his men had suffered so much since they had engaged in the siege he would be unable to guarantee our soldiers protection that General Garner's command should have. General Garner declined to accept his demand, saying that if he could take the fort we would risk the results. At daylight next morning Banks opened up on us with his artillery, and made a general charge by his land forces on our fort. We killed twice as many as our number, still defeating them at every point."[2]

The Confederate army was outgunned during the siege. Not only were they outgunned, but the Union army also was numerically superior on the battlefield. The disparity in numbers between the two opposing forces during the siege would be hard to demonstrate in other battles fought during the Civil War. This left Garner with very little choice but to devise a plan to neutralize the superior numbers Banks was able to field on the battlefield.

Confederate commanders displayed an uncanny ability throughout the Civil War to concentrate their limited resources against greater numbers during an attack. The strategy was highly effective in neutralizing a larger opposing army because it enabled Confederate generals to concentrate their strength at the point of attack with equal numbers. General Robert E. Lee demonstrated this during his campaigns in Virginia, and Garner had very little choice but to employ this tactic during the siege.[3] The small, beleaguered garrison was entrusted with the task of defending a complex system of earthen works that began at the river and encircled the fort, extending back into the river some miles below the fortress. Originally, Port Hudson's designers intended it to be defended by 20,000 men. When the Union fleet began the bombardment on March 14, the garrison's strength was close to these numbers. After Farragut's attack, a large portion of the garrison was ordered to relieve General Pemberton's garrison; he was hoping to restore his shaky position at Vicksburg at the expense of Garner's command. Garner used this type of strategy, shifting his scarce resources to the center of attack. Because he employed this tactic there were times during the siege when scarce manpower was spread so thin that other parts of the line were undefended. His line commanders were uneasy and protested in reports that they were left exposed to attack. Dissension surfaced toward the latter part of the siege and would lead to the arrest of one high-ranking line commander.

Tom Martin of Company G, 18th Arkansas Infantry further wrote, "There was not the snapping of the finger between the fire of the guns and the cannon. We held five miles of works day and night with continual loss of our forces. They made assault after assault upon our works, but we repulsed them every time. They dug up to our works so close that they could throw hand grenades over our lines, and the distance was so short that we were able to throw them back into their own lines before they would explode. They attempted to blow up our works at many points; we would concentrate at that point, and we defended them every time with great loss to them." He was describing the general assault on the works on the 27th by Banks, and in his report it is obvious that Garner was shifting his command, concentrating his strength at the point of attack.[4]

Steedman wrote a report to Garner on June 29: "The troops on the left wing are posted at the works in the following order, from right to left: Colonel Johnson's Fifteenth Arkansas, and Captain M. C. Peel's company, Eighteenth Arkansas; one brass 12-pounder howitzer, Captain A. J. Herod; two Blakely guns, two 6-pounders, First Lieutenant E. B. Thompson commanding; First Alabama, Major Knox commanding; Eighteenth Arkansas, Lieutenant Colonel Parish commanding; Tenth Arkansas, Lieutenant-Colonel E. L. Vaughan commanding; one 24-pounder siege gun (rifle); one 12-pounder howitzer and one 6-pounder gun, Lieutenant Toledano commanding; Thirty-ninth Mississippi, Colonel Shelby commanding; Wingfield Battalion, Major De Baun. At different points in Colonel Shelby's line are two 6-pounder guns, Captain Herod, one 6-pounder gun, Watson Battery, Lieutenant Caldwell commanding; one 6-pounder gun of Lieutenant Brown's ordnance department."[5]

Parish received orders to reinforce Lyles on the extreme right on June 30, 1863. The presence of the Arkansas troops there was short-lived, and they were soon sent back to Beall after the crisis had passed. Lyles wrote, "The 18th Arkansas has gone to General Beall. The little fight I think has pretty well blown over, though he is still making demonstrations. He got in my trenches and got one officer." The day before the Arkansas troops were sent to reinforce his position, Lyles had successfully repulsed an attack by the enemy, which he described as a feeble charge that left a number of Yankees dead and the remainder demoralized. By calling for additional troops to reinforce his position, he must have been anticipating a second charge.

There was no question that the Union fleet had suffered a loss at the hands of the Confederate gunners on March 14 while attempting to pass the fortified bluffs at night. The destruction of the <u>Mississippi</u> and the damage inflicted on Farragut's fleet was proof that any future attempt to run the rebel batteries would be met by stiff resistance. Even though Farragut did not completely execute his plan, he did manage to successfully place two warships above Port Hudson. His plan was clearly stated in an order he issued to his captains prior to running the batteries. "Captains will bear in mind that the object is to run the batteries at the least possible damage to our ships, and thereby secure an affected force above, for the purpose of rendering such assistance as may be required of us to the army at Vicksburg, or, if not required, to our army at Baton Rouge." The powerful war ship Hartford and her escort were now positioned to render assistance to both Banks at Port Hudson and Grant's campaign to reduce the stronghold of Vicksburg. It wouldn't take long before Farragut's plan began to produce dividends. The Union's ships intercepted a Confederate steamer on its way to replenish the garrison with a cargo of 300,000 pounds of bacon. Any other Southern ships that would attempt to run the blockade would meet with a similar fate.

Farragut's fleet and Banks with his land forces had shut down any hope of replenishing the fort's supplies, and they hoped to complete the stranglehold by capturing the Confederate stronghold by land. Towards the end of the siege, the Confederate army had exhausted its ammunition. The blockade caused the Confederate forces to suffer greatly. Putting innovation into place, they resorted to eating mules, horses, and rats to keep from starving.

Tom Martin of Company G, 18th Arkansas continued, "By this time our supplies of meat had been exhausted, and we then resorted to the slaughtering of mules and horses, which were boiled and served to the men for their substance the rest of the siege."[6]

With no prospects of replenishing the garrison's supplies, Garner issued orders to slaughter horses and mules for meat. Linn Turner Vince, stationed at Port Hudson wrote, "It was comical to see the facial expressions as they viewed the platters of hot steak fried in his own grease, or the chunks of boiled mule as it floated in a bucket of stew. However, there seemed to be perfect good humor as one after the other tackled the job, and numerous jokes and badinages were indulged and by the takers of the viands. Occasionally would some stalwart fellow throw back his head and utter a long and loud ye-ha, ye-ha, in imitation of a jackass or mule."[7]

I think it would be safe to assume that mule meat would not replace bacon with the traditional biscuits and gravy for a hearty morning breakfast to get a Southern boy started right just before he hitched his mules in preparation for the day's plowing to be done. Walking behind old Jed and Jack, watching the plow turn the earth, the smell of freshly tilled earth must have brought back memories of laughing and joking in order to keep their morale high during the siege and recollections of Johnnie Reb's first taste of mule meat.

Richard Stockton and Granville McGuire, along with the other soldiers, would have been called upon to utilize all existing resources available and to recycle those resources time and time again in order to extend the survival of the garrison during the siege. Stockton's thoughts must have been also focused on how much he loved Martha and their newborn son, born in September just before the Battle of Corinth was fought. He knew Martha and other Southern women were rationing and using whatever resources were available in order to survive. The sacrifices of their women could be one of several factors that accounted for the garrison's steadfast resistance to the end.

On June 20, the garrison began to run out of ammunition, and it became necessary to manufacture bullets, shells for the cannon, and other ordnance. The men were instructed to collect bullets, cannon shells that had not exploded, and mortar rounds that had been fired into the fort that were lying on the ground. Collecting ammunition became a daily routine during this phase of the siege. After the bullets were collected, they were melted down and in this way the Rebels were able to recycle the enemy's bullets. By using these innovative ideals they were able to make 4,000 to 5,000 Enfield cartridges daily and fire them back at Yankees.

My great grandfather Wilson Polk Wallace served as a private with a small detachment of Colonel Logan's 17th Arkansas Infantry inside the lines during the siege. The majority of Logan's 11th and 17th Consolidated served as a cavalry unit that operated outside Port Hudson, harassing the Union around Jackson, Louisiana, during the siege. His grandson James Newton Wallace remembers stories Wallace told him about how Confederates painted logs to resemble cannons, which deceived the enemy into believing they had more artillery than they actually had on the line. This was one of several ways the Rebels intimidated the Yankees by inflating their strength.[8]

Wallace was a typical Johnnie Reb who enlisted at age 17, trading his long-tailed shirts that were characteristic of his day for a gray jacket that would become worn and frayed with time.

Wallace and other soldiers experienced many nights sleeping on the hard ground, and oftentimes leaves, straw, or grass acted as a mattress, separating them from the dampness of an earthen bed. The average non-com during the siege often slept on the line awaiting the next Union attack. With a blanket made flimsy from many nights exposed to the elements, Johnnie would cover himself, hoping it might offer some warmth on a cold night. Wallace was caught in a snowstorm one night while serving in Mississippi. Wallace with a few other Johnnie Rebs, "took refuge in the gnarled, under the roots of a large tree in the forest. Falling asleep they awoke the following morning to find themselves warmly blanketed in snow and nearby tracks of Federals who had passed in the night." A soldier's knapsack would serve as a pillow. He would sometimes sleep under an open sky that might offer rain or snow. Johnnie Reb always hoped for a starry sky to serve as his tent, but didn't welcome the light from a full moon that might reveal his presence and invite a sniper's bullet.

He was proud of the gray jacket that covered his back, but as time passed the color would be changed to a faded buttercup brown. Johnnie's mismatched trousers were of different shades of blue and were issues of the United States Quartermaster Corps on loan to him, borrowed from an adversary who lay dead on the battlefield. Johnnie carried a United States Enfield rifle, which he captured from the enemy, and he was not concerned that his uniform was multinational. He especially took pride in his musket and bayonet by keeping them polished with moistened wood ashes. Johnnie had learned that in order to survive on the battlefield, he must prioritize and his weapon was one of his first priorities.

Captain Lewis J. Girard, chief of ordnance, would demonstrate that necessity is the mother of invention throughout the siege. He had the responsibility of maintaining the cannon, and because of his ideals the cannon continued to fire. Deadly accurate Union artillery fire had disabled most of the Confederate cannon at different times during the siege. By working nights, damage done to gun carriages was repaired, and guns that were dismounted were quickly remounted, ready for action by morning.[9]

Lieutenant Fred Y. Dabney was assigned to the Corps of Engineers and arrived at Port Hudson in the fall of 1862. He had the responsibility for strengthening the works and repairing damage done to the fortifications during the course of the siege. It was not unusual for a field engineer to lead troops into the thick of a fight during a battle. It is more than probable that Stockton's skills as a carpenter were fully utilized by the engineering officers. Because of the scarcity of men who were available to defend the works against a numerically superior onslaught of blue coats, I think it would be safe to assume that Stockton played the role of both defender and mechanic. This dual responsibility as builder and soldier must have added a measure of stress that ordinary infantrymen did not experience. The engineers had to repair the damage that was done to the fortifications or batteries, especially that caused by the Union artillery. Often repairs on the works required that they be made at night. Darkness lessened the chance that a sniper bullet might find its target. The work required long hours of laboring throughout the night, depriving them of sleep, and they were still expected to man the breastworks during an assault that usually would take place in the morning hours.

Dabney had earned his degree in civil engineering, graduating from Polytechnic Institute located at Troy, New York. He was a very skillful and resourceful engineer, which he repeatedly demonstrated during the siege. His Union counterparts had concocted a scheme that they hoped would undermine a Rebel salient. The Union moles had tunneled under part of the fortifications, hoping to blow the works to kingdom come. This type of warfare was developed by both North and South and would come to perfection during World War I.

Dabney was determined not to let the Union miners blow a few of his countrymen skyward and started digging a counter tunnel beneath them. The sound of the Union digging had alerted the Confederates to the location of the enemy tunnel. "Capt. Dabney tunneled beneath them, working in the shaft himself, with the sound of their picks over his head, digging the earth with trowels and sending it back in baskets. He tamped his charge with his own hands, not finding any one else willing to perform the dangerous service. When the Federal mine was about completed, he fired his mine by means of "friction primer", with a wire attached, passing through sections of cane to avoid the difficulties of angles in his small tunnel, and blew up the enemy before they were ready to spring their mine."[10],[11]

As the siege continued and progressed, the hardships of both Union and Southern soldiers also increased. The prolonged conflict increased the suffering of the men, and it was especially hard on the defenders, because as sickness and disease increased, those in need were deprived of the necessary medications to relieve their suffering. The defenders had no protection from the burning sun and were constantly exposed to the elements. They were constantly on alert. Both Union and Southern soldiers lived from moment to moment; each side had skillful sharpshooters who seldom missed, especially if a soldier was foolish enough to clearly expose any part of his body. Movements in the trenches had to be carefully choreographed, and snipers made the batteries untenable during the day. The troops were compelled to wait behind the fortifications for the next assault, and the constant wait created an uneasiness that eroded their nerves, especially among some of the officers who had the responsibility to defend their sector on the line.

The nutritional quality of their food continued to deteriorate, and by the middle of June supplies were quickly running out. All they had left to eat was cornbread and syrup, with a few peas that were ground into the cornmeal to make bread. The troops tried to forage for berries as much as possible if they felt they were safe from the snipers' bullet. They were under a constant threat of bombardment by the enemy's mortars and cannon, which shook the ground and rattled their nerves.

Most of the men at Port Hudson had arrived in October 1862, and had developed friendships with one another over a long period. There were only a small number of men who garrisoned Port Hudson, and over the long period they were stationed there they got to know each other by name, especially those who fought closely together on the line. The erosion of confidence by some of the junior officers during the very latter part of the siege was more of what appeared to be a family squabble than a hostile mutiny.

CHAPTER 12

Trouble on the Line

There was a problem that developed in Colonel Steedman's command which might have originated in his personality, caused by the constant emotional stress that he was under. The uncertainty of when his line might be breached was a constant concern, and it is remarkable that he didn't completely break down under this type of stress. It appears that Steedman was suffering from lack of sleep, for in a report he wrote, he stated, "I have not been able to close my eyes during the night. I am well this morning." This was in reference to an issue that he had with the 10th Arkansas Infantry. This was just before Banks ordered a general assault on the works on June 14. His report was dated June 11, 1863, and was written early in the morning, during sunrise. He went on to express in his report an uneasiness concerning an unreliable regiment, which occupied a threatened position on his left wing. Steedman wrote, "My only uneasiness is from an unreliable regiment which occupies the threatened point. It is impossible to remove them to-day. They are within 300 yards of a battery of six guns and two mortars. The reference to the regiment is an official secret. It is the Tenth Arkansas. I have had to conciliate them." He went on to write in the report that he wanted this matter to be kept secret because he felt it might spread to other regiments and cause problems.[1]

On June 11, he wrote another report that the enemy was preparing to attack his line at a point in front of the slaughter pen. He felt that Colonel Shelby's troops would be heavily engaged in this assault and had positioned the left wing of the 18th Arkansas around the battery at Bennett's house.[2] He expressed his confidence in the troops' ability to repulse an attack, writing, "Our men seem to be valiant, and in good moral condition in the mud and slop and surrounding circumstances will admit." In this report he was upbeat in his optimism of the deployment of the different regiments on the line and confident in their ability to hold their positions.

On the morning of the 11th, Steedman found the Tenth Arkansas still holding their position on the line. He wrote to Gardner, "Sir: Please say to the general that I found the Tenth Arkansas on the lines yesterday when I took command of this line. They had relieved the Twelfth Arkansas the night before. This plan of changing troops, except from necessity, is ruinous. I shall dispose of the regiments on this line to the best of my discretion, and keep them there. I gave such orders as I thought proper to effect this in last night, and all was moving smoothly until the Tenth Arkansas hesitated in its obedience to my order, and delayed the movement until the fight opened, so the whole movement was defeated." In his report to Gardner the fighting ability of the Arkansas troops was not at issue; he felt the officers were the problem: "They have no officers." He wrote to Gardner, "I feel no doubt, though, in reconciling everything to-day." He went on to reassure the general that his health was good, that he felt remarkably well that morning, and that he was confident in his health. The colonel was obviously under stress and trying to reconcile the issues with the Arkansas troops. The privates had proven that they would fight, and the issue might have been a personality conflict under the duress of battle with Lieutenant Colonel E. L. Vaughan of the 10th Arkansas.

When Banks ordered a general assault on the works on the 14th, the Arkansas troops played a major role in preventing Banks from carrying the works. All the troops on Steedman's left performed their duties valiantly, and without the coordinated effort of all the regiments present the Union would have taken the fortifications on the 14th.

On June 29, Steedman positioned Colonel Ben Johnson's 15th Arkansas, Colonel M. B. Locke's 10th Arkansas, and Colonel William Parrish's 18th Arkansas, as well as other units, on his left wing. The issue with the Arkansas troops began to surface again in his reports. He wrote, "I am greatly mortified and disappointed to report that about half the 18th Arkansas Regiment, 50 men, have refused to move to the right, as ordered, saying they have worked hard to fortify their present position."[3] Again Steedman was trying to reconcile this issue, reassuring the privates of the 18th that the assignment would only be temporary and that they could return to the positions they had fortified and worked on so hard. No doubt Grandpa was no fool and had worked hard, laboring to make their position impregnable, and they felt they could hold this position. In a few days the garrison would surrender, and stress was running very high among the privates; they knew surrender was just a matter of time. They were aware that their ammunition was fast being depleted and that the possibility of supplies being replenished was nonexistent. Parrish was prepared to go with those who were willing to follow Steedman's orders and report to Lyles' command.

On June 30, he reported, "About 80 men of the Eighteenth Arkansas are still in the trenches on the line. I have ordered them to move at once to the right, and join their regiment. They are under the command of Lieutenant." (Steedman asked that the remainder, those willing to go, to rejoin Parrish at his new assignment on the line. The question again was not whether the men were unwilling to fight. They were obviously still on the line prepared to fight unto death in order to repeal an enemy attack. They had not deserted that night; the issue was that they were confident they could defend and hold their fortified position on which they had labored so hard.

Steedman was fearful that they would lose Port Hudson to the enemy on the first vigorous assault against his line. Gardner had issued a communication, which was forward to the men in the trenches, stating, "This regiment should return as soon as the emergency is past." Gardner wanted to make the change permanent.

Steedman had reservations about this and said, "I would suggest if there is any safe position in which the regiment could be held in reserve, where they could be comfortable, it might prevent trouble." He felt there was prejudice in the 18th against Roe Colonel Lyles; roe possibly meaning rock-solid, or rocking. Steedman suggested to Lyles, "Perhaps an intimation to the colonel to be cautious in his orders to them might avoid difficulties." Steedman was hoping that any further trouble might be prevented on his line.

The Arkansas backwoodsmen were no fools, and they knew that the end was coming soon. They had many opportunities to desert in the face of the enemy. It can get oppressively hot in Louisiana in July. They had to be still in the trenches and on constant duty, waiting for any movement of the enemy. Being exposed to the direct sun with no relief and hot temperatures only added to their misery. When a thunderstorm would pass over, it would fill the trenches with water and turn the shell-shocked terrain into a sea of mud. The harsh, unsympathetic environment coupled with a diet that was destined to lead to scurvy would be enough to encourage desertion. "A Southern officer admitted that 150 went over to the enemy." He said these were almost entirely foreigners of a low class or ignorant conscripts from Western Louisiana." As the men from Arkansas were native born, almost without exception, they fell in neither class. Moreover, we have confirmation from the other side. "Many deserters came to us," wrote a Union officer, "mostly Louisianans, for the 'Wackerensackers' (Arkansas men) and the Texans rarely deserted."[5]

Lyles of the 23rd Arkansas was disliked by many of the privates who served under him. This might have been because he ruled with a heavy hand. The backwoodsmen and small farmers had carved out communities in a recent wilderness; Arkansas became a state in 1836 and was sparsely populated at that time of statehood. The Wackerensackers were pioneers, and many were independent. Some were sons of pathfinders who paved the way to a better tomorrow, bringing with them only the bare essentials that were necessary to survive in a primitive, unsettled world. Frontiersmen,

Ozark mountain men, fur trappers, and others running from the law would become the future explorers of what is now America. Some would become reluctant explorers: tarred and feathered, they would be driven from their secure communities back east and sent down river to the Arkansas Territory. Their persecutors felt they were sending them to a hellish environment and justice would be served. The Arkansas Territory was considered to be a swamp infested, hostile place of torment. They were partially right in their analysis, but not totally.

Vast herds of Buffalo numbering in the millions had roamed this lonely prairie, and when they were spooked by lightning, the earth would tremble by the pounding of their hooves upon the ground. It was a land filled with bear, deer, turkey, and panthers, with an abundance of small game for the taking. This is what the early pioneers saw on the prairies of southwestern Arkansas in what is now Hempstead County and in northwestern Arkansas. Many of the troops were self-reliant and had survived on the edge of civilization with two essential tools, a sharp ax and a strong back.

Both Steedman and Gardner agreed that the issue was with the officers and not with the troops. Gardner preferred consolation and diplomacy in dealing with the Arkansas troops. At no time were the fortifications in danger of being breached because of the stubbornness of these units.[6]

There is a possibility that Steedman was overreacting to the situation because of the stress coupled with the restless nights he was having. His reports reassured Gardner that he was in good health and was fit to command. It could be that he was having problems understanding the nature of the western frontier. Fred Harvey Herrington wrote in the Arkansas Historical Quarterly that, apparently excitable by nature, Steedman grew alarmed when several Arkansas soldiers refused to move into a new position. It was not mutiny, he was convinced of that, and he tended to assign the blame to company and regimental officers. Still, he was "greatly mortified and disappointed" at the developments and mournfully concluded that the men were, "loss to duty and state pride." In his closing arguments he was convinced that some of the Arkansas privates would have to be court-martialed and shot in order for the others to learn to obey orders, regardless of their own personal feelings. This was a few days before the surrender, and stress must have been at an all-time high.

Herrington continued to write, "There is a possibility that Steedman, in excitement overstated what he saw. He was not from Arkansas, and does not seem to have liked Arkansans very well. His letters show him a bit of an alarmist. His superiors, instead of using harsh, repressive measures, preferred consolation."[7] This was the policy of both Beall and Gardner in dealing with the issues.

Gardner had pulled troops from both Beall and Colonel W. R. Miles in order to reinforce other positions during June and early July. The issue of shifting troops to different points on the line with little regard for his junior officers' opinions began to surface in written protests. His policies were creating resentments that were beginning to mount in the closing days of the siege.

Miles wrote on July 6, just before the surrender, "Your order of today, directing me to retire the whole of Major Merchant's command, has been obeyed as well as that other order directing me to make a permanent detail of nine men from my command to report for duty to the provost marshal. In obeying these orders, however, I beg leave most respectfully to say that I think the public interest is greatly jeopardized thereby. Of the 125 men of Major Merchant's command originally given to me, the last is now taken away, and I am required to send away nine men in addition. This leaves me with less than 400 muskets to defend over 1-1/4 miles of breastworks. I have at least one-third of the entire line, and less than one-sixth of the fighting force to defend it with. Besides, when the center and left were in danger in the early days of the siege, the labor and blood of my command were freely contributed to sustain them. Now the right is sorely pressed, and most vigorously menaced than any other part of the lines, I hardly think it just to me, or right in view of public interest, to reduce my men to so low an ebb."[8]

A Confederate stationed at Port Hudson during the siege clearly understood the uneasiness the line commanders felt, because there were not enough fighting men to defend the place. He wrote, "The siege of Port Hudson was not more credible to the Confederates than it was discernible to the Federals. We had not enough men to make a good skirmish line around our four miles of works. At the time of any one of the assaults by the Federals, when the Confederates were centered at the point of attack, the thousands of Federal soldiers not engaged could have put their hands in their pockets and leisurely walked over the greater part of the ground embraced within our works."[9]

The issue of depleting one command at the expense of another was evident in a report that Beall wrote on June 8. "I would respectfully call the attention of major general commanding to the following facts; with my brigade I was assigned a certain portion of the breastworks to defend. Since the enemy having appeared on our front, more than one-third of my best troops have been taken from me and moved to the left, where they are now, under the command of a junior officer."[10] He went on to protest that Gardner had sent him men from another position that he had no confidence in. Beall felt he was better off without these men, and he recommended that they be watched and put under detention. All three of his line commanders had protested in reports expressing their dissatisfaction with his policy of indiscriminately shifting troops when it was not necessary, which they felt was causing problems, especially with willful junior officers.

Steedman had Lieutenant Colonel Vaughan arrested on July 7, two days before Port Hudson capitulated. Steedman wrote to Gardner, "In accordance with instructions from headquarters this morning, I have arrested Lieutenant Colonel Vaughan, Tenth Arkansas, and placed Captain S. M. Shelton, senior officer, in command. I can hear no bad effect resulting from rumors of to-day."[11] In the same report to Gardner he was reassuring and trying to keep it quiet as much as possible.

It might be interesting to take note that the fighting ability of the 10th Arkansas had been proven at Shiloh and at the siege of Corinth. The Arkansas privates established precedents at the hornet's nest that would be hard to equal in other fights. They were engaged along with the 9th Arkansas in the final assault on the hornet's nest where Brigadier Benjamin M. Prentiss' division had delayed the Confederate advance. They were aggressive during the attack on the hornet's nest and played a strong roll in taking this position. In the following report General Albert Sidney Johnson had a clear understanding of who the Arkansas frontiersmen were and knew that they would fight.

"The 9th and 10th Arkansas, fighting under General Breckinridge, were with the troops sent against Prentiss' division on the first day, meeting a destructive fire. There was a halt at the right of the line, and Governor Harris, of Tennessee, was addressing the men, when General Johnston rode up behind the Ninth Arkansas and asked that a file give way to let him through, at the same time requesting the name of the regiment. Being told, he turned, holding in his right hand a cup he picked up in a Federal camp, and facing the regiment, said with a smile, 'I want you toothpick men to show what you can do to-day!' The Bowie knife was called in jest 'The Arkansas Toothpick.' The enemy over there must be driven out. Will you help us to do it?" The electric current of this appeal thrilled the Arkansas men, and the answer was an enthusiastic dash and a rousing yell. Johnston rode with them, but the regiment passed him and carried the field. The fight was won! The Tenth regiment was next to the Ninth and went forward in the same headlong charge. Prentiss' division was taken, including no less than 3,000 men and the general himself."[12]

Steedman recommended harsh measures in dealing with the privates who wanted to remain at their fortified position and continue the fight. His solution to the problem was that some of the Arkansas soldiers would have to be shot following court-martial in order to convince the others that they must obey orders regardless of their own personal feelings. Shooting the privates appeared to be a desperate solution to a problem that did not warrant such drastic actions. Reason prevailed; Gardner obviously felt the arrest of Vaughan would put pressure on the offending, stubborn junior officers, compelling them to follow his orders regardless of their personal appraisal of his leadership.

On July 7 Vaughan was arrested--two days before the surrender. On that same day Beall expressed his concern about dissatisfaction in the ranks, "There is more discontent among the men within the last few days than I have discovered before, and I very much fear that the officers are at the bottom of it. If you have any corrections to give me in reference to use of troops in case the enemy gets over the works, I should like to have them, as I do not think his attack will be delayed much longer, as his works are very formidable and to appearance, nearly complete. But one company of the 10th Arkansas has reported, the others refuse, so I am told."[13] Time was running out for the gallant defenders of Port Hudson. They had fought so long and hard, holding onto a small piece of real estate on the Mississippi, with a hope that their struggle would prevent Banks from joining Grant at Vicksburg. They had accomplished their goal, proving that a few good men could fight for so long under the most adverse of circumstances and leave the fight with their heads held high.

Gardner's chances of winning against such great odds were marginal, and he was aware of this. Time was running out for the gallant defenders of Port Hudson. They had fought so long and hard, holding onto a small piece of real estate on the Mississippi, with a hope that their struggle would prevent Banks from joining Grant at Vicksburg. They had accomplished their goal, proving that a few good men could fight for so long under the most adverse of circumstances and leave the fight with their heads held high.. There was no question that he had performed his duty well and was ready to hand over his sword, knowing in his heart that he and his men could leave their posts confident they had resisted to the end. Gardner knew that Federal reinforcements would soon be arriving from Vicksburg, which would further strengthen Banks, and he knew there was nothing left but to yield to these hard realities.

On July 7, Banks consulted with his officers to make the final preparations for the last assault. A storming party of 1,000 Union volunteers was organized to breach the battered fort defenses. Heavily charged mines were put in place at the siege works, which would signal the final doom for the exhausted defenders. Fortunately for those brave men of both North and South, a note was dispatched to Banks, informing him that Grant had taken Vicksburg.

The struggle had to end; Gardner stated that he was willing to surrender the garrison. He wrote, "Having defended this position as long as I deem my duty requires, I am willing to surrender to you, and will appoint a commission of three officers to meet a similar commission appointed by yourself at 9 o'clock this morning, for the purpose of agreeing upon and drawing up the terms of surrender, and for that purpose I ask for a cessation of hostilities."

As the good news spread throughout their trenches, I can hear the jubilant shouts of the Union army poised for the final attack. A note was quickly dispatched to the Confederate works. I can hear the shout by a Johnnie Reb saying, "That's just another damned Yankee lie." But the Rebels must have known, because the forest echoed with the strains of the "Star Spangled Banner" from a long-silenced band. As the firing died away, silence fell upon both lines, North and South. The next morning at 2 a.m. the long-awaited gray envelope came from the commander of the besieged defenders, admitting surrender.

"But, stout as the defense had been, the besiegers had on their part displayed some of the highest qualities of the soldier; among these valor in attack, patient endurance of privation, suffering, and incredible toil, and perseverance under discouragement. And to the defenders and besiegers it is alike unjust to say, even though it has been said by the highest authority that 'Port Hudson surrendered only because Vicksburg had fallen.' The simple truth was Port Hudson surrendered because its hour had come. The Garrison is literally starving."[14]

On July 8 a long train of supplies was dispatched to the famished garrison. Final preparations were made for the surrender. On July 9 the Union army marched into the fortress with colors flying and bands playing. The Confederates stacked their arms and hauled down their flag, and in its place flew the Stars and Stripes. By order of Banks, Gardner's sword was returned to him in the presence of his men in recognition of a heroic defense. Stockton and McGuire were paroled at Port Hudson and made their way back to Saline County. On their way back both men must have thought about the events that had brought them to Port Hudson.

CHAPTER 13

Trip Back Home

Richard Stockton had a lot of things to think about on his trip back to Saline County. The persuasive enthusiasm that had influenced both McGuire and Stockton, motivating them to rally behind the Southern cause, had found its rest in a soldier's grave near Holly Springs. A lawyer is trained to present his arguments before a court, convincing all that his case is right. The student lawyer George Isaacs would never be able to defend a client before a jury or persuade a legislative body to pass a bill. Stockton was living with the Isaacs in Saline County in 1860 and was listed on the census as a student. As students they must have had many long conversations, expressing their hopes and expectations for a better Arkansas. Almost all young people have dreams of how their presence in the future might change things to come. Perhaps Isaacs shared his hopes with him that someday he might run for public office and serve his country well. Isaacs' death was realized as a personal loss to Stockton and McGuire, who served under him. It was a tragic loss because of what he might have become, a good citizen of Arkansas.

They must have thought about the many who died of measles and those who were sent back home sick on the first march together to DeValls Bluff and the families that would mourn their loss. They had not fired a shot at the Yankees, but their track was marked with the graves of stricken comrades whom they had to bury, and death's victory would deny their chance of becoming good citizens. On arriving at Fort Pillow sickness and disease continued to reduce their numbers. Stockton must have become increasingly conscious of the hard realities of the war and the suffering and hardships that were yet to be faced. They had to evacuate Fort Pillow because the price to defend the fortress was too high, and he must have thought about that on his trip north to Arkansas.

At Corinth, Mississippi, the regiment continued to lose numbers to sickness and disease. At Iuka after all the hard training and discipline they had gone through they experienced a disappointing loss to the Yankees who they thought they could easily whip. Stockton's obituary states that his mind dwelled on things of the future, and it must have become increasingly clear to him that it would be a long, hard fight before they would return home as conquering heroes.

The casualty rate his regiment experienced at Corinth was equal to any loss in any other Southern regiment in battles that were yet to be fought throughout the South. Stockton served under Colonel John Daley and must have admired and respected him. It's possible he might have witnessed on the battlefield his death and the deaths of other officers of Cabell's brigade. The losses there were horrendous, and there were only a few of his friends and fellow soldiers who were left to defend Port Hudson when they arrived there in October. Stockton and McGuire were no longer green recruits, but were seasoned veterans who had proven to themselves that they would fight for what they felt was right, and if they had to look back they would have no regrets because they knew they had fought the good fight against impossible odds.

The two men must have painfully understood the consequences of the fall of Port Hudson. They had firsthand knowledge, experienced at Port Hudson, of the severe penalty that would be imposed upon the South by closing commerce and communications on the Red River. Farragut had succeeded in placing two warships above the fortress, which prevented the garrison from being reequipped. The Red River was a vital artery that furnished the Confederacy beef cattle, grain from Taxes, sugar, salt from Louisiana, and European goods that were shipped into Mexico and destined for the Red River. They were aware that Port Hudson defended the southern anchor and Vicksburg defended the northern anchor, both of equal importance in keeping the lifeline open. They must have been fully aware that plans were under way by Union strategists to complete the stranglehold by taking possession of the Arkansas River and the state capital at Little Rock. Their farms were located 25 miles south of the capital, and events were about to transpire that would bring the war to their back yards.

The officers were sent to prison camps after the capitulation on July 9, 1863, leaving the enlisted men without leadership. The Federals paroled 5,935 men, who included civilian employees, and out of the 6,800-man garrison Gardner's losses included 188 killed, 483 wounded and 200 who died of sickness and disease. The imprisonment of the officers was done purposely by the Federals; this was done to break the close emotional ties, bounds of trust, and respect that were formed during combat and hardships experienced while serving together. Both men might have decided not to rejoin the 18th because their regiment, as they knew it, no longer existed. After returning to Saline County, Stockton signed an oath of allegiance, pledging his loyalty to the Federal government on December 31, 1863, at Pine Bluff, Arkansas.[1]

Oath of Allegiance

I, Richard T. Stockton, of Calvert J. S., County of Saline, State of Arkansas, do solemnly swear that I will have true allegiance to the United States and support and sustain the Constitution and Laws thereof; that I will maintain the National Sovereignty paramount to that of all State, County or Confederate powers; that I will discourage, discountenance, and forever oppose Sedition, rebellion, and the disintegration of the Federal Union: that I disclaim and denounce all faith and fellowship with the so-called Confederate Armies, and pledge my honor, my property, and my life in the sacred performance of this my solemn oath of allegiance to the Government of the United States of America.

Certificate:

Sworn to and subscribed before me, this the (Signed Richard T. Stockton) thirty-first day of December, A.D. 1863, at Pine Bluff, Arkansas.[2]

Not only was the garrison starving during the siege, but it was also true that many families of the beleaguered defenders were equally suffering back home. Both Stockton and McGuire had mouths to feed and crops to plant. They had proven that they could stand in the face of death and adversity. Their critics would be hard pressed to challenge a record of unwavering bravery in the face of the enemy and the highest conduct soldiering can achieve during the longest siege in American military history that kept 40,000 Union besiegers at bay for nearly two months. Stockton's thoughts were focused on the future, and by signing the oath of allegiance he must have been fully committed to rebuilding their lives with Martha and their newborn son, who was born while he was on duty. McGuire must have had similar thoughts also, for he had an even greater stake in the future--he was the father of five children.

By December 1863 the men knew that Vicksburg had fallen to General Grant and that Robert E. Lee had suffered a devastating defeat at Gettysburg, which had forced the proud Army of Northern Virginia to limp back to Virginia.

I don't know what time of day it was when Richard finally could see his house in the distance. I can almost hear the dogs barking and yipping, signaling to the family inside that their long-awaited master was finally home.

Stockton's obituary states that his mind dwelt on things of the future. Perhaps when he signed the oath of allegiance he was thinking of the Bible verse, "...this one thing I do, forgetting those things which are behind, ands reaching forth unto those things which are before, I press toward the mark for the prize of the high calling of God in Christ Jesus."[3]

The following obituary appeared in the <u>Arkansas Methodist</u> May 29, 1897.

"His companionship was calculated to make a man better. His conversation was always of something practical and elevating. His mind dwelt much on things of the future and his end was that of a quiet and unassuming Christian soldier, laying aside his armor for a crown. He was as devoted a steward in his church, as we ever knew. He was as charitable a Mason as we have ever met. He was a true and devoted a friend as could be found anywhere. His life was one of earnest solicitude for the welfare of his children and friends. His death is realized as a personal loss by the editor, and all connected with the <u>Headlight</u>. Grant County has lost one of her best citizens. The Methodist Church one of her steadfast friends and supporters. The Masonic fraternity one of its most zealous and charitable members. His family a father who's every heart throb was a prayer for their good in life to come. Farewell, friend and brother.

"We clipped the above from the <u>Sheridan Headlight</u>, edited by Brother J. S. Williams, who had known Brother Stockton for many years. Brother Stockton was born September 11, 1836. Moved to Arkansas in the fifties and settled in what is now Grant County. He formerly belonged to the Baptist Church, but joined the Methodist Church under the pastorate of Rev. C. Pope, in 1859. He was married to Miss M. L. Isaacs September 5, 1860, with whom he lived happily until she preceded him to the heavenly home a few years before his death.

"On March 23, 1897, he laid aside his armor, which had been kept bright by the work he wrought in trying to promote the cause he had espoused in the days of his vigor and manhood of youth. He was regarded as the pillar of New Hope Church, near Sheridan, where he had held his membership--serving as steward a good portion of the time--for nearly forty years. He leaves 8 children, six sons and two daughters. May his noble mantle fall upon his sons. O. H. Beadle"[4]

CHAPTER 14

The Hardships of Southern Women

Elizabeth Isaacs

The Confederates were in control of Little Rock during the Corinth campaign. It wouldn't fall into possession of the Union army until September 1863 when General Steele advanced upon Little Rock, captured the state capital, and further complicated the lives of the Isaacs family.

Newspaper publications, such as the True Democrat and the Arkansas Gazette were still being published at the time of the siege of Corinth. Letters and soldiers returning home were some of the main sources of information along with stories and accounts relating to the war printed by local newspapers. Newspapers were able to get information relating to the war quicker, this being made possible by the invention of the modern telegraph. Telegraph lines were of vital necessity, not only for the Confederate government, but for the Federal government as well. From Richmond, Virginia, the center of communications for the Confederacy, to the trans-Mississippi theater of war, which encompassed a vast expanse of land stretching over 1,000 miles, the telegraph was indispensable.

It became a priority by both governments to keep these lines of communication open at all cost. Special units were assigned to accomplish this goal. If telegraph poles were not available, or the resources to erect them, then wires were strung through trees and even brush was used as a temporary solution to ensure open communications. As the war progressed, it was demonstrated that the usefulness of the electric telegraph became indispensable. Quoting from an article entitled "The Military Telegraph," "One phase of life in the telegraph room of the war department was Lincoln's daily visit thereto, and the long hours spent by him in the cipher room, whose quiet seclusion made it a favorable retreat both for rest and also for important work requiring undisturbed thought and undivided attention. There, Lincoln turned over with methodical exactness and anxious expectations the office file of recent messages. There he awaited patiently the transitions of ciphers, which forecasted promising plans for coming campaigns, told tales of unexpected defeat, recited the story of victorious battles, conveyed impossible demands, or suggested inexpedient policies. It was one of the deciding factors in winning the war for the Union especially in the use of tactical operations. This along with the railroad enabled the Union army to move large numbers of troops to the battle field quickly."[1]

Major General Hinman issued General Order No. 2 from the Headquarters of the trans-Mississippi District in Little Rock on June 2, 1862. This order dealt with a list of those persons who were exempt from the draft. Order No. 7 dealt with the classifications and occupations that would be exempt from conscription: persons actually engaged in carrying the mail, one ferryman at each ferry on every post route, and telegraph operators actually employed as such. It was important to the Confederate authorities in Arkansas that communications were kept open, and they were making every effort to keep them from being disrupted.[2]

The Isaacs women knew their husbands were in Mississippi with Sterling Price's Army of the West and that a build up of scores of Arkansas troops had left the state and crossed the Mississippi River. It wasn't clear to many Arkansans why there was a military mobilization that depleted the state of troops needed to defend its borders. Many felt that the Confederate authorities in Richmond had abandoned Arkansas and had left her defenseless. In spite of their reservations the women were making every effort and sacrifice to help in the war effort while their husbands were away. These efforts were focused on hard labor and long hours of toil in trying to keep the family together. They had to continue to manage the crops and livestock while the men were absent. This must have compounded their worries. I'm sure they were anxiously awaiting news and letters from their husbands who were far from home.

McGuire was the father of four children, and the uncertainty of not knowing whether their daddy would ever return must have been constantly on their minds. The 1860 Census of Saline County lists the names of his children as James M. McGuire age about 8, Shara A. McGuire age about 6, Isaac McGuire age about 4, and Charles G. McGuire age about 4. It must have been difficult for Naomi to deal with their inquisitive questions concerning Daddy. I can almost hear the children ask, "Mama, where's my daddy? I want my daddy, and when is he coming home?" while tugging on her apron like all children do who are trying to get their mother's attention.

The answer to the question of why he joined the Confederate army at age 28 has always eluded me. Their youngest child, George Washington Grandville, was born in 1860 and was less than one year old when McGuire joined the service. It is more than probable that Naomi was nursing little George at the time of his enlistment. McGuire joined in March 1862; this was before strict draft laws were enforced in the state. It is more than probable that he held strong beliefs in the Southern cause and was realistic enough to know by then that joining would disrupt his family, and there was a possibility Daddy would not return alive to see them again.

According to McGuire's military record, soon after joining the 18th he was sent home sick. He was absent for nearly a year. His body may have been weakened by the measles epidemic that devastated the 18th. He eventually regained his strength and returned to duty at Port Hudson, Louisiana. Returning home sick soon after he joined must have increased Naomi's hardships. It was difficult enough trying to take care of the farm, and the burden of a sick husband compounded her difficulties.

McGuire left for his assignment in Tennessee before the draft was enacted. When Hinman took command of the trans-Mississippi, most of the Arkansas troops had left with Van Dorn and Price during the buildup below Corinth. Hinman inherited a command on paper only, with no army to prevent the Union general Curtis from advancing on Little Rock. He was determined to strengthen the defenses of Arkansas and did so by strict draft enforcement laws. He had planned an offensive in northwestern Arkansas and needed manpower to carry out his strategy. Confederate forces under Van Dorn had evacuated Washington and Benton Counties after their defeat at Pea Ridge, March 8, 1862. Hinman hoped to recapture that part of the state. The strict enforcement of draft laws in Arkansas was met with resentment and didn't advance the Southern cause. Martial law was declared in the state, and it eventually degenerated into forced conscription of men and boys into the Southern army. Hinman was very unpopular in Arkansas, and after the citizens of the state mounted protests and outcries he was replaced.

The capture of New Orleans by Admiral Farragut effectively shut down the flow of commerce the South was depending upon. New Orleans was located near the mouth of the Mississippi River and bordering her banks were four important Southern states. The Mississippi River represented the jugular vein of the South, which was dependent upon the states of Arkansas, Tennessee, Mississippi, Texas, and Louisiana for a continuous supply of conscripts and volunteers to fill the ranks of the Confederate army. These four states, plus Texas, were responsible for raising large numbers of soldiers that gave the Confederacy an effective fighting force. Not only was the region a continuous supply of manpower vital to the Confederate cause, but Richmond also was dependent upon the cotton grown in these states to clothe the backs of her army. The supply of cotton in the five states was sufficient to meet her needs throughout the war, and it became ever clearer to the Federal government the necessity of shutting down this lifeline.

New Orleans was the largest city of the South and retained a large industrial base that had the capacity to furnish the needed resources to wage an effective modern war. Within this base of enterprise could be found machinery workshops that were capable of casting heavy guns and of manufacturing rifles. New Orleans had a ship building industry that had the capacity to build ironclads and other naval vessels that could be used in the war effort. The city was a center of trade and commerce, importing from England goods and supplies that were not manufactured in the four states of the Mississippi River Valley.[3]

The closing of the lower Mississippi River by Farragut's fleet had immediate positive results for the Union cause. The seizure of the port had far-reaching consequences for the South and in time would strangle her efforts to continue the struggle.

Because of the blockade the women of the Confederacy had to improvise with whatever resources were available. In the early part of the war this inspired Southern women to band together and pool resources. Communities of women--literally this was the case, for all able-bodied men were in the service--would come together to pool their resources in order to keep the war effort alive. Small cottage industries sprang up that were operated by women who were determined to furnish whatever was necessary for their men who had gone to battle. Women worked at looms, tanneries, and spinning wheels to ensure a continuous flow of supplies to the army. They gathered herbs, such as horehound, mullein, and boneset to furnish much-needed medications for the sick and wounded. The women cultivated poppy plants for medicinal purposes. When the plants reached a certain stage of maturity, they cut the stock. They then collected sap from the plant and dried it. This process was used to manufacture opium that was shipped to hospitals and doctors in the field. Opium was one of the principal painkillers used to relieve the anguish and suffering of the wounded during the Civil War.

Indigo was used to dye clothing, and if a woman was fortunate enough to own a pair of candle molds she would use beef tallow to mold candles for use by the troops in the field. Boxes were sent to camps that might contain shoes, homemade handkerchiefs, pin cushions, needles, sewing thread, soap for washing, and homemade blankets made from carpets taken from the floors of their homes. Soap was also used to prevent their feet from blistering on long marches.

Boxes of different descriptions were sent containing red pepper that was used for seasoning food and for sprinkling in a soldier's sack in order to keep his feet warm in winter. Packages contained homegrown rice, linens made from tablecloths and pillowcases, roles of bandages made from the bed linen, brown paper that was highly prized, along with goose quills for pins, and bottles of homemade ink. Anything was sent that might make better the life of the soldier who was exposed to extremes in the weather and who lived in primitive conditions in the camps. There were boxes especially prepared for the wounded and the sick, containing delicacies such as coffee and tea that were hoarded and stored in secret places to prevent hungry armies from forging and taking these valuable treats from them.[4]

Most of the South was an agrarian society, and families were more dependent on each other for their survival, more so than we are now. South central Arkansas was a recent wilderness that had been opened for settlement in the early 1840s. Not only were families dependent upon one another, but they were also interwoven together to form self-sufficient communities. The very fabric of Southern society was being eroded by the absence of Southern men and by torrents of destructive events that were undermining the foundation of Southern life that would never quite be the same again.

As the war progressed and hardships increased, the women's thoughts focused on caring for their young children, especially on where the next meal was coming from. It wasn't unusual for a family to go to bed hungry without anything to eat. There were constant threats that even though the corn crib was full in the morning, that might not be the case by evening. There was no assurance that their food sources were safe, for the age-old drama of hungry forging armies with ferocious appetites could quickly deplete their scarce resources and stores of the commodities they were dependent upon. Longing to tell their husbands how much they missed and loved them and reaching to the other side of the bed to find it empty would be disheartening. Perhaps many of them cried themselves to sleep fearful of a stranger's knock on their door at night, but pioneer women were tough and very resourceful. If I were that stranger I would be hesitant to knock, for many of the pioneer women were dead shots with the pistol and rifle and wouldn't hesitate to use them in defense of their family and children.

Mrs. D. I. Vance wrote the following letter describing her hardships during the Union occupation of Little Rock, Arkansas. Her letter can be found in the Garland County library located in Hot Springs, Arkansas. It is interesting to note that she lived not too far from where the Isaacs lived. The communities she described, such as Princeton and Arkadelphia, Arkansas, were a short distance from Cherry Grove, now Crossroads. We can only speculate if there was a possibility that Vance knew the Isaacs. Vance lived 20 miles below Little Rock. The location of her farm south of Little Rock would place her in the near vicinity of the Isaacs' farm at Cherry Grove. Hartwell Reynolds is my third great grandfather and had enlisted in Company G, Monroe Arkansas First Cavalry. Captain Vance was Reynolds' commanding officer. Elizabeth Isaacs was Silas and Sarah's oldest daughter and was married to Reynolds. The fact that the husbands of both Mrs. Vance and Elizabeth enlisted in Monroe's Cavalry would increase the probability that Elizabeth stayed in touch with Mrs. Vance concerning news about the war and the fate of Reynolds.

"Hardships of the wife of a captain in Monroe's Regiment"
by Mrs. D. L. Vance of Eureka Springs.

"My husband, D. L. Vance, was captain of Company G., Monroe's Regiment, Cabell's Brigade. He went to the army the first of the year 1862, and remained in it till he was killed by Union home guards, July 1864. I lived in the country, about 20 miles below Little Rock. After the Federals took Little Rock it was not long until they began foraging through the country. Several of them passed my house one day, and when they came back they had a drove of cattle. The road ran through our field, and they had two large gates to pass through. Some of my cattle had just come up and I went to drive them out of the way and got all away but one, when the

100

Yankees drove it away from me. I was so angry that I threw the club I had in my hand at one of them. I tried to hit him, but struck his horse in the face; I got a cursing for it. The gentleman said he would run his bayonet through me if I did that again.

"A few Negroes were still with me. I had hired them to gather my corn, and they had just started in with a load when they met the Federals. The Negroes had a yoke of oxen to the wagon, and the soldiers made them take the oxen out, and they drove them off with the other cattle, and the Negro men returned to the house.

"I was sitting on the front steps seeing it all. He came up to me and said, 'You ought not to have struck that man's horse; that's what made them take the oxen.' I said I did not care: they had taken nearly all I had, and I would as soon die as live.

"There was a young paroled soldier, a neighbor, and he went to their camp that evening and pleaded with them to give up the oxen, but the lieutenant, a very gallant gentleman, said they would not and sent word to go and he would tell me what he thought of me. I did not go to find out.

"At another time I was away from home a day or two, and when I returned, the first thing I saw was the top of my corn crib tore off. I knew what that meant. The Federal soldiers had been there in my absence and taken nearly all my corn.

"One time my husband sent his horse home with a very sore back. I doctored him and fattened him. He was a fine riding horse. One day I was sitting at my window and saw two soldiers coming through the field. I went out the back hall door where I could see the horse in the horse lot. I was afraid they would take him. I stood there some time and did not see the Federals pass. I stepped back to the hall door and there they stood in the hall. They said, 'What did you get up from the window for? Your husband is home and you went out to tell him to hide.' I replied, 'He is not at home.' They said they knew better, and that was what I went out for. It made me so angry I said, 'I don't tell lies, and if you want to know what I went out for it was to see if you were going to take my horse.'

"They went to the horse lot and looked in his mouth, and when they came in again they said, 'You need not hide that horse tonight.' I told them I was not going to hide him, but I knew they were going to take him, so when I got up the next morning I went out to look for him and he was gone. They did not take him out through the gate, but let the fence down at the back of the lot.

"The same paroled soldier that tried to get them to give up the oxen followed them ten miles the next morning and pleaded so hard they gave them up. Well, I sent for this young man and he went to the next house about a mile from my house where the wagon train had stayed that night. There was a plantation of corn there that the owner had run off and left as soon as the Federals took Little Rock. The ground was frozen and I could hear the train going before we got there, and when we got there everyone was gone but the one who had my horse, and he was just starting. I rode up to him and said, 'That's my horse. What are you going to do with him? I want my horse.' I was determined to follow him to Little Rock if he did not give him up. He eyed the young man with me, for he had a gray uniform on. Once the fellow put his hand back on his gun, but he did not scare us. We stood there quite awhile. I kept telling him to give up my horse, so at last he gave him to me, saying to the young man, 'She's got a brudder-in-law that put the devilment in her head.'

"That was my husband's brother, Captain J. M. Vance, that came with Steele's army. I went home with the horse and took a little nephew and went to Little Rock. I rode the horse. We did not overtake the wagon train until we got to the arsenal. I got a pass to go south and went home and got a little boy to go with me.

"We started to find Monroe's Regiment. I heard it was at Arkadelphia. I rode that horse, for I was determined the Federals should not have him. We were a long way and heard the Regiment was at Princeton, so I went there. I inquired in the town and they told me the Regiment was camped at the edge of town. After two or three days and news came the Federals were coming, and our boys hustled out. I told the boy that came with me we would meet the Federals, but he must not tell them which road the soldiers took.

"Sure enough, we had not gone far until we met them. An officer asked us how far we had come. I told him. He then asked if any Rebel troops were there. I told him 'no' then he wanted to know when they left and what road they took. I told him I did not know. He spoke very crossly, and said, 'It is very strange, Madam, you do not know.' Then he turned to the boy and spoke crossly to him, and he got scared and said they went down the Camden road. I left the horse with my husband and rode a sore back pony that belonged to the Negro man my husband had with him.

"A set of vagabonds sprang up as soon as the Federals took Little Rock. They went to General Steele and told a tale of woe about how they had been treated, and he let them form companies. They call themselves home guards. My husband and two of his men were on a scout and were slipped upon by those men and shot. He was killed and one of his men was wounded and a boy who had taken them some papers was shot, while telling him not to shoot him that he was no soldier, but they shot him and badly wounded him."[5]

In the summer and fall of 1862 a flood of volunteers flocked to the enlistment centers, volunteering for service in the Confederate army in Arkansas. This was largely due to conscription laws that were being strictly enforced. Every white male between 18 years old and 35 years old was given a choice of volunteering or facing the possibility of being drafted. There were stigmas associated with conscription. Southern men preferred to volunteer, for they felt it was a disgrace to be drafted. I think this played a major role in the decision-making process that Hartwell Stain Reynolds employed. He volunteered for service in Monroe's Arkansas First Cavalry at Pine Bluff, Arkansas, and enrolled as a private on June 16, 1862, to serve from October 1, 1862, through April 30, 1863. Volunteering for service gave him an option to choose which branch of the service he wanted. This preference for service was quite apparent by the large number of volunteers for cavalry service. So many units were formed that it would be necessary to dismount cavalry units, redesignating them to infantry regiments. I believe this preference for cavalry duty was the case with my third great grandfather Hartwell Reynolds. Becoming a horse soldier appealed to the frontiersmen who had to learn to ride and shoot at an early age in order to survive.[6]

Colonel James Code Monroe commanded Monroe's Arkansas First Cavalry. Monroe was one of the most colorful figures in the trans-Mississippi department of the Confederate forces. He was a well-known figure in the western division as the ragged colonel of "The Rawhides," because he refused to live better than the conditions his men were experiencing. If the regiment was short on rations and his men went hungry, he would not eat. If his men were poorly clothed, he wouldn't wear anything better than they had. Monroe had a well-earned reputation as a cunning adversary and was referred to as "The Terror" by General Steele.[7]

Reynolds was ordered to Mulberry, Arkansas, which was being used as a staging ground for campaigns in northwest Arkansas.[8] Mulberry is located on the Arkansas River. The Confederate army was using Mulberry or Fort Smith as a landing to unload supplies that were shipped up the river. His official military record states he was detailed to report to D. B. Clark at Mulberry, and he was marked absent on the muster roll. This period of the enlistment was from October 1, 1862, to April 30, 1863. The record also states he was issued a horse and a gun. During this time frame the regiment participated in the Battle of Cain Hill and then fought the Battle of Prairie Grove near Fayetteville, Arkansas.

Hartwell died in camp somewhere in Franklin County. This info can be found in Elizabeth's obituary on Page 3 of the Arkansas Methodist, dated April 26, 1884. Another source of information is from William Forrest Reynolds. William was born May 9, 1886, in Rye, Arkansas, and lived close to Henry Reynolds, Elizabeth's father-in-law. Henry died of pneumonia on November 24, 1887, at age 78. Henry's plantation was located south of Rye in Hurricane Township, Bradley County, Arkansas. William knew many of Henry's descendants personally. He had firsthand knowledge of the family and had access to the Family Bible Records.

The following is a letter written by Hartwell Reynolds while serving with (Monroe's) Arkansas Calvary. This was the last letter the family received before he died. He was on his way to Yellville, Arkansas, but Monroe's orders were changed and he was ordered to Fort Smith to stop a union advance on the city. Hartwell was sick while traveling with his cavalry unit and somewhere in Franklin County he died in camp. The family Bible records list the cause of his death as the flux. I can only speculate as to the time he died while stationed in northern Arkansas. The letter was dated Sept. 24, 1862. Company G's first major engagement was Cane Hill, fought on November 27, 1862, and then Prairie Grove fought on December 6, 1862. In the letter he states his condition as improving and because of this, he might have been well enough to have participated in these battles and then died later.

Soldier letter H. S. Reynolds
A private in Capt. Davis
Fagans' Regiment

Des Arc Sept. 24,1862

Dear Lizzie,
I embrace the present opportunity of writing you a few lines. I have been a little unwell but am improving. I hope the few lines will find you all well. I have no particular more to write you. I recon you hear more then I do. We will start in the morning to Yellville. We are taking the field every day. I don't think that we will have much more fighting to do. I just written you a few lines because we are going away. Address your letters to Pine Bluff. No name at the present. I am ever yours affectionately.

H. S. Reynolds
The decision for Hartwell to enlist in the Confederate army must have been a difficult choice for Elizabeth and Hartwell to make. The 1860 Census of Bradley County, Arkansas, lists their four children as Leonidas age 5, Erasmus age 2, and Mary age 1. Silas C. was born August 12, 1861. When his father enlisted on June 20, 1862, Silas was less than 1 year old. There is a good possibility that his mother was still nursing him. Elizabeth was 34 years old at the time of his enlistment and wasn't considered a young woman,

because the life expectancy in 1862 was less than it is now. Her obituary states that she struggled with the storms of life, but always kept her faith in Christ. I can well imagine how hard it must have been on her when she lost Hartwell and was left to raise three boys and one girl. Arkansas had been depleted of most of its economic resources, the most precious being those loved ones who were killed and would never return. The economic burden was further intensified by the many who would return wounded or crippled from the war and would never be able to work again. The economy of the South was left in shambles and would not fully recover until the Second World War. Elizabeth was truly facing a bleak future, with four young children to raise by herself, and there were not many good prospects for marriage available.

She knew it would be difficult to manage the farm without the help of her husband. The casualty rate during the Civil War was horrendous, and Arkansas experienced one of the highest death rates. Her prospects of finding strong, able-bodied men to help her work on the farm didn't look too promising.

I am not trying to suggest that her situation was hopeless, because Elizabeth was a pioneer woman and she was cut from a breed of self-sufficient, resourceful women who learned to survive at an early age on the western frontier. She was living close to her father-in-law, Henry Reynolds, and Hartwell had several brothers who might have been able to advise and assist in the management of the farm. There was a Methodist Church and a fellowship of believers in the community that she could have depended upon.

One of the first acts of early Methodist settlers in the Rye community was to establish a place to worship God and a school to educate their children. A schoolhouse built of logs served as a meeting place until a church could be erected, which was also made of logs cut from the abundant forest near by. Some time no later than 1845 the Union Methodist Church was organized at Rye. After the Civil War, a larger church was constructed of lumber and served the congregation until about 1940, being replaced then with the present-day structure. Henry and Nancy Reynolds were charter members and donated the land for the church. Many of their descendants are buried in the Union Cemetery, located across the road from the church. It is more than probable that the people in her community pooled their resources to rebuild their lives and to recapture their dreams that were inspired by the early morning sunrise that pointed to the western horizon.

Elizabeth Isaacs was no exception to the common denominator: faith in Christ that influenced the lives of her parents. In researching the documents associated with the Isaacs family, I found records that go back 150 years. Their faith in Christ clearly stands out and reoccurs throughout the historical record they left. I would like to have known them personally; discovering these records has been an inspiration to me.

"Our Church at Lakeside, Pine Bluff, has again been bereaved by the death of one of our best women, in the person of Sister Elizabeth E. Reynolds, who was in the 66th year of her age. Our sister's maiden name was Isaacs. She was married to Hartwell S. Reynolds, whose body now fills a soldier's grave, having died in camp during the late war, leaving her with three sons and one daughter to battle with the storms of life, which she nobly did. Having in her early life taken Jesus into her life he did not desert, but stood by and gave a helping hand. Her life was one of devotion to God. Her religion was her strong support, and when death came she was ready, talking of her funeral and its management as but a short journey. Sons and daughters, you can afford but to live for your mother's heaven."

John F. Carr
Pine Bluff, AR[9]

I can't write with absolute certainty concerning the past, and most historians would agree that the mosaic profile we try to reconstruct with bits and pieces of information could only reveal a misty silhouette from yesteryear. Two different biographical writers using information for brushes would paint different pictures of the personalities they hoped to reveal. I have always been intrigued with Martha Isaacs Stockton, and in my mind's eye and heart I have an image of how she should be. I would like to think that she was a beautiful woman, and I can see her tresses floating in the breeze as she waved goodbye to Richard on his departure to Fort Pillow.

A good description of Richard Stockton can be found in a document he signed entitled "Oath of Allegiance to the Federal Government" which he signed after returning to Saline County. In order to regain his citizenship, the Federal authorities required Stockton to sign an oath in which he pledged not to take up arms against the United States and agreed to oppose all rebellion aimed at the disintegration of the Federal Union. Stockton stood six feet tall and had a fair complexion, brown hair, and blue eyes.[10] Information obtained from his obituary gives a colorful description of his character, which provides insight into what he stood for, such as honesty, dependability and a willingness to give of his time for the betterment of his community. Stockton held the office of Steward in the Methodist Church, was a member of the Masonic Lodge, and had gained the respect of the community in Grant County when he died.

I can say with certainty, based on information obtained in my research, that the Isaac women married men of high moral character. In order for them to attract men of this caliber, they must have radiated true beauty that comes from a spirit of faith and devotion to God. Martha L. Isaacs was about 24 years old when she married Richard on September 5, 1860. Twenty-four years of age was somewhat late for a woman to marry during this period. This phenomenon occurred throughout the records; all the Isaacs women married in their early to mid 20's. Perhaps they were exercising good judgment by waiting for that special person who could fulfill their hopes and dreams. I'm sure that among the criteria they set for following that special person in life's journey together was that he must be a follower of Jesus Christ.

According to Stockton's official military record, he enlisted in the Confederate army in July 1862. Virgil was their first-born son and was less than 1 year old when his father enlisted. It is interesting to note that their second child, Richard Randoff, was born on September 21, 1862. This was just before the ferocious battle that was fought at Corinth in October which resulted in extremely high casualties for both the North and the South. Martha and Richard were married less than two years when the Arkansas 18th Infantry marched off to war, leaving her pregnant with the care of a small child. These circumstances only reinforce my first thoughts of what she might have been. Now I can see in my mind's eye Richard embracing Martha and reassuring her that he loves her and would soon return victorious. Now the mosaic changes as the misty past departs; we see him waving goodbye to Martha as he boards a train leaving for the battlefield. I am sure she is holding a young child in her arms, and it is obvious to all that she is carrying one yet to be born. I have always thought that pregnant women were beautiful because they carry the gift of life. The historical record that reveals in part further reinforces Martha's beauty.

Richard and Martha's family tree gives us another clue to Martha's character. On examination of the tree we find that they were blessed with nine children, six boys and three girls. They were born in a time frame between 1861 and 1870. The economics of large families in our modern world is prohibitive because of the financial burden associated with raising children. During the 1800's, large families were necessary and looked upon as a premium, ensuring the success of the family farm with a continuous supply of labor.

Martha must have had a deep devotion to her parents because she named three of her sons after her brothers and one of her daughters after her youngest sister. Silas Stephen, born in March 1865, was named after her father, Silas Isaacs. Addison L., born June 8, 1868, was named after her brother Addison J. Isaacs. George L., born October 22, 1871, was named after her youngest brother, George W. Isaacs. James L., born August 21, 1875, was Martha's youngest son and was named after her oldest brother, Dr. James L. Isaacs.

RosAltha Alice, born March 9, 1870, was named after her youngest sister, RosAltha D. Isaacs. During this era it was a tradition to carry on the family name by naming descendants after family members.[11] I'm sure the tradition played a role in this, but it also would be safe to assume she was trying to express her love and devotion to the memory of her family.

The fall of the Rebel strongholds at Vicksburg, Mississippi, and Port Hudson, Louisiana, set in motion a series of unfortunate events for the Confederate cause. The defense of the trans-Mississippi Theater was dependent on keeping open the vital arteries of the Arkansas and Red Rivers. Fortunately for the Confederacy, the material resources in Texas were left relatively intact. Much needed supplies flowed down the Red River from the west and cattle were herded overland. The fall of Port Hudson and Vicksburg had the same effect on these two important waterways as the closing of the Port at New Orleans by Admiral Farragut's fleet.

The Northern strategists fully recognized that the control of the Arkansas River was necessary to prevent any future Southern designs on northern Arkansas and Missouri. The Confederate garrison at Vicksburg surrendered on July 4, 1863, to General Ulysses S. Grant, and soon after that a plan was devised by the Union high command to seize Little Rock on the Arkansas River. Major General Frederick Steele was ordered to Helena, Arkansas, and was given command of all the Union forces in Arkansas. Steele was a subordinate of Grant and had participated in the capture of Helena, Arkansas, and Vicksburg. They became acquainted with each other at West Point, and both graduated from the Academy in 1843.

On August 10, 1863, Steele left his base at Helena and began to move his army of 6,000 in the direction of Clarendon on the White River. The plan was to rendezvous with Brigadier General John Davison's cavalry that was moving south from Missouri. Disease is no respecter of persons, especially when an army is moving through swamp-infested terrain. More than 1,000 of Steele's troops became sick on the march to Clarendon. Hoping to find relief and a healthier base of operations, he moved to DeValls Bluff.

On September 2, 1863, Steele arrived at Brownsville, which was close to present-day Lonoke. There he joined Davison's cavalry, which had preceded him. With reinforcements and Davison's cavalry he had a combined strength of nearly 14,500. Word of Steele's advance had preceded him and rumors spread, causing panic in Little Rock and the areas surrounding the city. The war in Arkansas and Missouri was mean-spirited. It was only a matter of time before Steele's army would be roaming the countryside, taking possession of anything valuable that they could find. Junius N. Bragg, a Confederate surgeon, while traveling from Pine Bluff to Little Rock wrote in a letter to his wife, "The country from here to Pine Bluff is the poorest most God forsaken country I have seen in Arkansas. No one, scarcely, lives on the road; all the little farms are deserted, and the people gone. They have fled long since from the supposed advance of the enemy, and starvation."[12]

The defense of the city of Little Rock was assigned to Major General Sterling Price. Price had about half the number of men that Steele had. Price was facing two dilemmas: not only was he understaffed, but he also had to deal with petty rivalries that were tearing his general staff apart. Two members of Price's high command, General Marmaduke and General Walker, had a simmering feud that erupted as Steele advanced on Little Rock. Rumors reached Walker that Marmaduke had accused him of cowardice in the face of the enemy as they retreated from Helena, trying to stop Steele's advance. Amazing as it might seem, the two generals settled their difference in a duel, which resulted in the death of Walker.

In spite of these compounding difficulties, Price tried to fortify the city with his limited resources. His efforts proved to be fruitless. The Confederate army had to abandon the city in September 1863, and the state capital was moved to Washington, located in Hempstead County. The capture of Little Rock had immediate consequences for the Isaacs of Saline County. They were now at the mercy of the Federal occupation army and had no recourse but to resign themselves to martial law. Their everyday activities were under scrutiny by provost marshals, and in order to travel out of the county they had to receive permission to do so. The scrutiny must have been intensified because Silas Isaacs had two sons who were officers in the Confederate army.

Martha Stockton was about 27 years old when Federal troops captured Little Rock. Richard and Martha had several options at their disposal that could be employed in order to protect the family from impending lawlessness. They must have been alerted to the fact that hordes of hungry Union scavengers were descending on Saline County. Martha's sister Elizabeth Isaacs lived in Bradley County, which was located 30 miles south of her. The Confederate government retained control over most of south Arkansas throughout the War. This part of the state would become a safe haven for refugees fleeing from the Federal advance. They might have chosen to remain in the county, relying on Stockton's parole. He had pledged not to rejoin his unit and resume hostilities against the Federal government. The signing of the parole was necessary in order to procure his release after the surrender. If this were the case, they would have to depend on the good faith of the provost marshals to honor his parole.

I believe Silas had died at the time Steele took the state capital. In a transaction Silas and Sarah sold a parcel of land in Saline County on April 22, 1861, to son James. James sold and deeded land to Sarah on May 25, 1861, according to Page 252, Book G, Saline County probate records. County tax records were disrupted by the Civil War and stopped in 1863. In 1863 Sarah was paying taxes on land she owned, and this would indicate Silas was no longer alive, for Sarah was the head of household and conducting business. Somewhere between 1861, when they were recording land transactions, and 1863, when the taxes were last payed on properties in Saline County by Sarah, Silas had died. I don't know what caused his death. It's possible he simply died because of the hardships and grief created by the war. Grant County was created from Saline County in 1868. Silas is not recorded in the 1870 Census of Grant County. The Grant County courthouse burned to the ground some time before the turn of the century, destroying all the records. This has complicated my research because all the probate and will records were destroyed in the fire.

Mrs. O. M. Mashburn of Saline County wrote the following letter. She was living in Saline County when General Steele took the city. She was an eyewitness to what happened and gives a firsthand account of what took place in the county.

"I am now 78 years old. I was born in Georgia, but moved to Arkansas in 1863. My husband's home at the opening of the Civil War was in Saline County. Our little children and my brother, Tom Bell, made our home a happy one. My husband and brothers soon joined the Confederate army and went through the war safely.

"When the Federals came to Little Rock, scouting parties raided Saline County. The havoc and destruction cannot well be described. At the time we had plenty of stock, horses, cows, and sheep and hogs. They took everything, even cutting the cloth from the looms, taking bed quilts and all clothing, except what the family was wearing at the time. Bread and water were our diet for many long stretches of time. They set fire to the house and cursed us for putting it out. It was a dreadful time.

"My husband came home on furlough just after the Federals had begun their raids. On one occasion my husband was not watchful enough and they caught him. In some way they had heard that he had money hidden in the house. They hung him with his own bridal ranks, leaving him half-dead."[13]

A large percentage of Arkansas men were enlisted in the Confederate armies during the Civil War. It has been estimated that all over, seven-eights of the able-bodied men from Saline County and the surrounding area joined to fight for the Southern cause. The recruiting and organizing of Confederate units from the vicinity left the county depleted of young men by the latter part of 1862. Before Steele took Little Rock in September 1863 the region was populated by old men, young boys, women, slaves, and disabled or wounded Confederate soldiers who had returned from the front lines and were no longer able to fight. This left the entire area in a state of perpetual stress because there were no healthy men to work the land, only women and some slaves who remained loyal to their owners.

After the fall of Little Rock, disenchanted Confederates began to drift back into Saline County, and many clearly felt that the fall of Vicksburg and the defeat of Lee at Gettysburg signaled the war would soon be over and there was little hope left for Southern independence. Some of these returning Confederate soldiers organized squads of Union sympathizers, which were called gray-backs. These bands of marauders acted as vigilantes in the county, raiding those families who had men still in Southern service.[14]

Lieutenant James L. Isaacs was one of many disabled soldiers who returned to Saline County. After he fully recovered from his illness he resumed his medical practice there as a civilian.

Little Rock would stay under Federal control for the remainder of the war. Steele held the capital, but the countryside was subject to periodic raids by gorilla bands and raiders based in southern Arkansas until the end of the war.

The Civil War was the bloodiest struggle in American history, and it can truly be called a holocaust that left the Southern states in ruins. The conquest of the South decided once and for all the fate of the nation. Brother fought against brother and father against son. It was also a war where mothers struggled to keep the family alive with a hope that there would be a better tomorrow after the terrible struggle ended. I believe that they were the first to see that the price paid was too high in human tragedy, and many must have said to their men, "Come home, for we too have paid the price."

EPILOGUE

Jenkins Ferry: The Final Battles in Saline County

The Battle of Jenkins Ferry would prove to be one of many battles during the war where the resources of Southern communities close to the conflicts would be taxed to their limit. Jenkins Ferry is located on the Saline River a few miles southwest of the little community of Cherry Grove where the Isaacs lived.

The battle was fought on April 30, 1864, and was the last in a series of fights that took place during the Camden Expedition. The Confederates fought the Union army at Wolf Creek, Elkins Ferry, Prairie De Ann, Poison Springs, Mark's Mill and finally at Jenkins Ferry. The campaign began on March 23, 1864, when Major General Frederick Steele's Union columns left Little Rock on their ill-fated drive, hoping to link up with General Banks in Louisiana, and ended with the Federals retreating back to Little Rock the first week in May, much wiser.

Banks left his base at Grand Ecore, Louisiana, and moved up the Red River in a two-pronged attack, hoping to join Steele at Shreveport. The Southern army met his advance at Mansfield and finally at Pleasant Hill. These two engagements would spoil his plans to break up the western Confederacy. Banks was hoping to crush General Richard Taylor's southern army, which would open the way for a conquest of Texas.[1]

The Confederate victory at the Battle of Pleasant Hill, Louisiana, on April 9, 1864, proved to be the decisive turning point in ending the Red River Campaign. Even though Taylor's Southern forces had to withdraw from the battlefield at Pleasant Hill, the Confederate victory was measured as a success because it prevented Banks from any further encroachment into western Louisiana and Texas. Banks was persuaded to withdraw his expeditionary force because of the determined resistance of Taylor's numerically inferior army.

The divisions of General Thomas J. Churchill's Arkansas and General Mosby M. Parson's Missouri troops, who had fought at Pleasant Hill, were sent by General Kirby Smith to reinforce Sterling Price after the Battle.[2] Price had gained victories over Steele at Poison Spring and Mark's Mill, stopping

Steele's columns from advancing any farther south than Camden. Steele tried to regroup at Camden and waited there for reinforcements to arrive from Pine Bluff with supplies. On the way to Pine Bluff the Union wagon train encountered the Confederates at Mark's Mill. The Rebels destroyed part of Steele's empty wagons and captured many that were trying to break out of the trap. He waited for more reinforcements, but his train was unable to break through. With very few options left he decided to retreat and march his troops back to Little Rock.[3]

Churchill's and Parson's reinforcements arrived on the battlefield in time to help pursue the retreating Federal army that had run out of supplies at Camden. Kirby Smith had personally taken command of Confederate forces, and the combined armies joined in an attack as Steele's forces tried to cross the Saline River. Fresh from a victory in Louisiana and fighting on home ground, the reinforced Rebels were determined to intercept the Yankees and trap them at the river. Fleeing and discouraged, the main body of Steele's army reached the banks of the Saline River and found the river swollen from recent rains.

Steele's engineers managed to build a pontoon bridge across the river in spite of the fact it had overflowed its banks and was flooding the Saline River bottoms. The floodplain had become filled with muddy waters, creating a murky swamp with floodwaters flowing though stands of timber that had formed a natural barrier and would prove to be an ideal location to defend against the Confederate pursuit.

Struggling through deep mud, Steele managed to get the main body of his army across the river. He left a contingent of about 4,000 men under the command of General Salomon to act as a rear guard, hoping to delay the Confederate advance and safely escape.[4] With the largest part of his men and wagons across the river on the north side, he quickly ran into more trouble because the ground was soggy and his train bogged down in the swampy ground on the other side. By the time he reached high ground there was no question that Johnny Reb had put the scare on the Yankees, for they were fleeing in utter disarray.

Eager to lighten his load and to travel as quickly as possible, Banks gave orders to abandon the remainder of his wagons. By the time the Federals reached Little Rock, those columns that marched into Little Rock had little more than the shirts on their backs. Old Woodpecker, Sterling Price, had a good opportunity at Jenkins Ferry to entrap the retreating Union army. It was his intention to surround the Yankees, which he did, and then to cut off their retreat. If he had been successful in his plan, it would have left Arkansas wide open for Confederate operations and would have given Price an opportunity to reoccupy Little Rock.

The Union rear guard needs to be given credit for preventing a total disaster; without their determined resistance on the south side of the Saline all would have been lost. The guards were positioned north of Cox Creek, concealed behind logs and trees in the bottom. Smith's Confederates attempted to attack the center while the remainder tried to overcome the rear. After entering an open field and exposing themselves, the Rebels soon found themselves at a disadvantage, for they began to take casualties from the Yankees who were waiting to deliver a deadly cross-fire. After fighting hard, the Federals managed to retreat across the river, then destroy the pontoon bridge as soon as they reached the north side of the river.

This action prevented the Southern army from nipping at the Yankees' tucked tails and capturing Steele's battered army. Unfortunately for the Yankees, in their haste to get across the river they had to leave part of their dead and wounded where they fell, along with a large amount of wagons and supplies.

The Second Kansas Colored Infantry played an important role in preventing the Confederates from completely routing the Yankees. During the earlier Battle of Poison Springs, the colored regiments suffered very high casualties, numbering about 500. The Negro troops were determined not to let this happen again, and this accounts for the ferocious fight they put up. The Second Kansas was the last regiment to leave the battlefield, leaving only after the Confederates had disengaged the attack and had withdrawn from the field.[5]

Jenkins Ferry is within a few miles of where Doctor James Isaacs, Richard Stockton, and James McGuire lived. The families in the area must have been aware that a major fight was taking place near their homes. Large troop movements were passing through the countryside near their farms, and the sounds of cannon and musket fire could be heard in the distance. They knew from experience that the wounded would have to be taken care of by the civilian population after the fight was over.

For three days after the battle, Union troops were overrunning the countryside, and citizens near the battlefield were unable to assist or help the wounded who lay in the field during this period. It was a time of uncertainty for those who were seriously wounded and needed immediate care. The people of the communities near the battlefield anxiously waited for a safe opportunity to enter the landscape where death and carnage had taken place. Some of the wounded were taken to a hospital at Tulip to be cared for.[6] Others were cared for in homes and buildings that were close to the battlefield. Some of the wounded were left at New Prospect Church near Sandy Springs to be cared for.[7] The countryside was littered with the remains of Steele's fleeing army, leaving in its wake burned wagons with the contents destroyed and scattered along the track to Little Rock.

It is quite ironic that the final major campaign in Arkansas would take place in their own backyard, about eight miles west of the Isaacs family's farms in what is now present-day Grant County, Arkansas. The anxiety of not knowing whether this would be a Confederate or a Union victory added to their concerns. I am sure they thought, "Will the Yankees take a stand in the surrounding fields of freshly plowed crops that have recently been planted?" I am sure they wondered, "Will the victor take the spoils?" They knew from experience that armies have to be fed. The people had reservations about the next occupation. Would it result in more hardships or reprisals against those who were sympathetic to the Union cause? By now, there were many who felt the war for Southern independence was a lost cause.

After the Camden campaign the war in Arkansas began to wind down. Martial law replaced civil authority after the Federals took Little Rock, beginning the period of reconstruction in northern Arkansas, starting in 1863 and ending in 1874.

General Richard Taylor, commanding the Department of Alabama, Mississippi, and East Louisiana, surrendered his Confederate forces at Citronelle, Alabama, on May 4, 1865, nearly two month after Lee's surrender at Appomattox Court House. The armies of the trans-Mississippi Department under General Kirby Smith ceased hostilities and negotiated terms of surrender that were approved on June 2, 1865, at Galveston, Texas.[8]

Kirby Smith's was the last major Confederate force to surrender, and some of his officers refused to capitulate, choosing instead to regroup in Mexico, hoping to continue the struggle. This was the case with the Ragged Colonel of the Rawhides, James Monroe, who could never say to his men that they were whipped, but chose instead to become a refugee in exile. In his last letter written from Mexico he expressed a desire and longing to return to Arkansas, eager to see his family and friends once more. He was disgusted with the wickedness, corruption, and violence of his surroundings and was repulsed by the cruelty exhibited during the bullfights. One of his comrades who left the country with him returned to the United States to report that he was killed trying to keep the peace in San Luis Potosi. He was young, 27 years old; perhaps if he had lived longer he would have changed his mind and come home.[9]

Dr. James L. Isaacs continued to practice medicine in Grant County until, like his early pioneer father, Silas, who moved west, he too followed the early morning sunrise that called to him to follow its journey across the sky to a new beginning beyond the western horizon. Leaving an impoverished Grant County in 1884, he moved his family to Hadley, Texas, located in

Tarrant County, close to Fort Worth, Texas. Following in the footsteps of his father, he settled near a community of Wesleyan believers and a center of education and learning. The following is his obituary.

Fort Worth Record, Thursday Morning, February 22, 1917

"Dr. J. L. Isaacs, 90, 3214 Avenue G., Polytechnic, died Wednesday night at his home. He is survived by a daughter, Miss Elizabeth, and a son Lonnie Isaacs. Funeral services for Dr. Isaacs will be held at 3 o'clock Thursday afternoon at the Polytechnic Methodist Church and interment will be in Greenwood. Rev. E. B. Hawk, assisted by Dr. J. P. Mussett and Dr. C. M. Hutton will officiate. The Masons will have charge of the services. Dr. Isaacs was born in Alabama and spent a part of his early life in Mississippi, coming to Hadley, Texas, in 1884, from where he moved to Polytechnic several years ago."

My great grandfather Wilson Polk Wallace was a member of Colonel James C. Monroe's First Arkansas Cavalry and fought in all the battles during the Camden campaign. Wallace served under General Nathan Bedford Forrest's Cavalry in Mississippi and fought there until the end of the war. Unlike Richard T. Stockton, who signed an oath of allegiance in 1863, Wallace was a diehard Confederate who refused to capitulate and would not swear allegiance to the United States Government until the carpetbagger government was thrown out of office in 1874, after which he signed the oath of allegiance. Quoting from an article about his life which appeared in the Arkansas Gazette in 1938, "Age changed his attitude towards the war. Like others of his youth he felt the Civil War was the right way to settle the trouble, but in old age he affirmed that war is evil and wrong and that slavery was never right. He had no theories as to how war can be prevented, but he felt that every possible means should be affected to prevent it."[10]

APPENDIX 1

18th Arkansas Assignments 1862 to 1864
O.R.-- SERIES I--VOLUME X/2 [S# 11] Page 463

CONFEDERATE CORRESPONDENCE, ORDERS, AND RETURNS
RELATING TO OPERATIONS IN KENTUCKY, TENNESSEE,
NORTH MISSISSIPPI, NORTH ALABAMA, AND SOUTHWEST
VIRGINIA FROM MARCH 4 TO JUNE 10, 1862, #7

Organization of the Army of the West, Maj. Gen. Earl Van Dorn commanding,
April 29, 1862

JONES' DIVISION

Maj. Gen. SAMUEL JONES

First Brigade

Brig. Gen. A. RUST
18th Arkansas, Colonel Carroll
20th Arkansas, Colonel King
19th Arkansas, Colonel Smead
Jones' Arkansas battalion
Lemoyne's Arkansas battalion
McCarver's Arkansas battalion
--- Battery

O.R.-- SERIES I--VOLUME X/1 [S# 10]   Page 790

APRIL 29-JUNE 10, 1862--Advance upon and siege of Corinth ...No. 38.
-- Report of Col. William P. Johnston, Aide-de-Camp and Special Inspector,
in reference to operations in Department No. 2.

Confederate States forces, General Braxton Bragg commanding, Army of the
Mississippi, June 30, 1862

Third Division

Brig. Gen. D. H. MAURY

First Brigade

Col. T. P. DOCKERY.
18th Arkansas Regiment
19th Arkansas Regiment
20th Arkansas Regiment
McCarver's Arkansas Battalion
Jones' Arkansas Battalion
battery

O.R.-- SERIES I--VOLUME XVII/1 [S#24] Page 376

OCTOBER 3-12, 1862, Battle of Corinth, Miss., and pursuit of the
Confederate forces. No. 104, Organization of the Confederate Army of West
Tennessee, Maj. Gen. Earl Van Dorn commanding, at the battle of Corinth

PRICE'S CORPS, OR ARMY OF THE WEST
MAURY'S DIVISION

Brig. Gen. DABNEY H. MAURY

Cabell's Brigade

Brig. Gen. W. L. CABELL
18th Arkansas
19th Arkansas
20th Arkansas
21st Arkansas
Jones' (Arkansas) battalion
Rapley's (Arkansas) battalion
Appeal Battery

O.R.-- SERIES I--VOLUME XVII/2 [S# 25] Page 734

CORRESPONDENCE, ORDERS, AND RETURNS RELATING TO
OPERATIONS IN WEST TENNESSEE AND NORTHERN MISSISSIPPI

FROM JUNE 10, 1862, TO JANUARY 20, 1863CONFEDERATE CORRESPONDENCE, ETC.--#6

Organization of the Army of the West, Maj. Gen. Sterling Price, C. S. Army, commanding, October 20, 1862

Third Brigade

Col. J. E. CRAVENS
16th Arkansas
18th Arkansas
19th Arkansas
20th Arkansas
2lst Arkansas
Adams' Arkansas Battalion
Hobbs' Arkansas Battalion
Jones' Arkansas Battalion

O.R.-- SERIES I--VOLUME XXIV/3 [S# 38] Page 614

Correspondence, Orders, And Returns Relating To Operations In Mississippi And West Tennessee (And Those In Arkansas And Louisiana Connected With The Siege Of Vicksburg) From January 20 To August 10, 1863

CONFEDERATE CORRESPONDENCE, ETC.--#1

Organization of the troops in the Department of Mississippi and Eastern Louisiana, Lieut. Gen. John C. Pemberton, C. S. Army, commanding, January 31, 1863

DISTRICT OF LOUISIANA

Maj. Gen. FRANKLIN GARDNER

Beall's Brigade
27th Alabama
31st [49th?] Alabama
6th Alabama Battalion
11th Arkansas
14th Arkansas
15th Arkansas

16th Arkansas
17th Arkansas
18th Arkansas
23rd Arkansas
1st [8th] Arkansas Battalion
1st Mississippi
39th Mississippi
1st Mississippi Light Artillery

O.R.-- SERIES I--VOLUME XV [S# 21] 1033

Confederate Correspondence, Orders, And Returns Relating To Operations In West Florida, Southern Alabama, Southern Mississippi, And Louisiana From May 12, 1862, To May 14, 1863: And In Texas, New Mexico, And Arizona From September 20, 1862, To May 14, 1863.--#12

Organization of troops in the Third Military District, Department of Mississippi and East Louisiana, Maj. Gen. Franklin Gardner, C. S. Army, commanding, March 31, 1863

BEALL'S BRIGADE

Brig. Gen. W. N. R. BEALL
11th Arkansas, Col. John L. Logan
17th Arkansas, Col. John L. Logan
12th Arkansas, Col. T. J. Reid
14th Arkansas, Col. O. P. Lyles
18th Arkansas, Col. O. P. Lyles
23rd Arkansas, Col. O. P. Lyles
15th Arkansas, Col. B. W. Johnson
16th Arkansas, Col. B. W. Johnson
8th Arkansas Battalion, Col. B. W. Johnson
1st Mississippi, Col. J. M. Simonton
39th Mississippi, Col. W. B. Shelby
1st Mississippi Light Artillery, Battery B, Capt. A. J. Herod
1st Mississippi Light Artillery, Battery F, Capt. J. L. Bradford
1st Mississippi Light Artillery, Battery K, Capt. George F. Abbay

O.R.-- SERIES I--VOLUME XV [S# 21] Page 1062

Confederate Correspondence, Orders, And Returns Relating To Operations In West Florida, Southern Alabama, Southern Mississippi, And Louisiana From May 12, 1862, To May 14, 1863: And In Texas, New Mexico, And Arizona From September 20, 1862, To May 14, 1863.--#13

Organization of Troops in the Third Military District, Department Mississippi and East Louisiana, commanded by Maj. Gen. Frank. Gardner, April 30, 1863

BEALL'S BRIGADE

Brig. Gen. W, N. R. BEALL commanding
49th Alabama, Col. Jeptha Edwards
1st Arkansas, Battalion, Lieut. Col. Bart. Jones
11th Arkansas, Col. John L. Logan
17th Arkansas, John Griffith
12th Arkansas, Col. T. J. Reid
14th Arkansas, Col. F. P. Powers
18th Arkansas, Col. R. H. Crockett
23rd Arkansas, Col. O. P. Lyles
15th Arkansas, Col. B. W. Johnson
16th Arkansas, Col. David Provence
1st Mississippi, Col. J. M. Simonton
39th Mississippi, Col. W. B. Shelby
Company B, 1st Mississippi Light Artillery, Capt. A. J, Herod
Company F, 1st Mississippi Light Artillery, Capt. J. L. Bradford
Company K, 1st Mississippi Light Artillery, Capt. George F. Abbay

O.R.-- SERIES I--VOLUME XXIV/3 [S# 38] Page 707

Correspondence, Orders, And Returns Relating To Operations In Mississippi And West Tennessee (And Those In Arkansas And Louisiana Connected With The Siege Of Vicksburg) From January 20 To August 10, 1863

CONFEDERATE CORRESPONDENCE, ETC.--#5

Organization of the troops in the Department of Mississippi and Eastern Louisiana, Lieut. Gen. John C. Pemberton, commanding, April 3, 1863

Third MILITARY DISTRICT

Maj. Gen. FRANKLIN GARDNER

Beall's Brigade

Brig. Gen. W. N. R. BEALL
11th Arkansas
17th Arkansas, Col. John L. Logan
12th Arkansas, Col. T. J. Reid, jr.
14th Arkansas
18th Arkansas, Col. O. P. Lyles
23rd Arkansas
15th Arkansas
16th Arkansas, Col. B. W. Johnson
1st [8th] Arkansas Battalion
39th Mississippi, Col. W. B. Shelby.
1st Mississippi Light Artillery, Batteries B, F, and K

O.R.—SERIES I—VOLUME XXVI/1 [S# 41] Page 144

MAY 21-July 8, 1863, Siege of Port Hudson, La.
No. 32. Statement of Confederate organizations paroled at Port Hudson

1st Alabama, Col. I. G. W. Steedman
49th Alabama, Maj. T. A. Street
Maury (Tennessee) Artillery
1st [8th] Arkansas Battalion, Lieut. Col. B. Jones
10th Arkansas, Maj. C. M. Cargile
11th and 17th Arkansas (detachment)
12th Arkansas, Col. T. J. Reid, jr
14th Arkansas, Lieut. Col. Pleasant Fowler
15th Arkansas, Col. Ben. W. Johnson
16th Arkansas, Col. David Provence
18th Arkansas, Lieut. Col. W. N. Parish
23rd Arkansas, Col. O. P. Lyles
4th Louisiana (detachment) Capt. Chas. T. Whitman
9th Louisiana Batt'n (Infantry), Capt. T. B. R. Chinn
9th Louisiana Battalion (Partisan Rangers), Maj. J. De Bann
12th Louisiana Heavy Artillery Battalion, Lieut. Col. P. F. De Gournay
30th Louisiana (detachment), Capt. T. K. Porter

Miles' (Louisiana) Legion, Col. W. R. Miles
Boone's (Louisiana) battery, Capt. S. M. Thomas
Watson's (Louisiana) battery, Lieut. E. A. Toledano
1st Mississippi, Lieut. Col. A. S. Hamilton
39th Mississippi, Col. W. B. Shelby
Claiborne (Mississippi) Light Infantry, Capt. A. J. Lewis
1st Mississippi Light Artillery (three batteries)
English's (Mississippi) battery, Lieut. P. J. Noland
Seven Stars (Mississippi) Artillery, Lieut. F. G. W. Coleman
1st Tennessee Heavy Artillery, Company G, Capt. James A. Fisher
1st Tennessee Light Artillery, Company B, Lieut. Oswald Tilghman
Improvised Tennessee Battalion, Capt. S. A. Whiteside

PORT HUDSON, LA July 5, 1863

O.R.—SERIES I—VOLUME XXXIV/1 [S# 61] Page 785

MARCH 23-MAY 3, 1864--The Camden (Arkansas) Expedition.No. 49. --
Organization of the Confederate forces in Arkansas, General E. Kirby Smith
commanding, April 20, 1864

DISTRICT OF ARKANSAS
Maj. Gen. STERLING PRICE

Dockery's Brigade

Brig. Gen. THOMAS P. DOCKERY
12th Arkansas Battalion Sharpshooters
18th Arkansas
19th Arkansas (Dockery's) Lieut. Col. H. G. P. Williams
20th Arkansas

APPENDIX 2

Record of Events for 18th Arkansas Infantry (Confederate)

Field and Staff

David Williamson Carroll, Col., r. August 25, 1862
John N. Daly, Lt. Col., to Col., died October 5, 1862
Robert Hamilton Crockett, Maj., Lt. Col., Col.
William N. Parish, Lt. Col.
Samuel H. Southerland, Maj.
Craven Peyton, Surg.
Flowers McGregor, A.Q.M.
Abraham Furst, A.C.S.
Eugene Henderson, A.S.
William S. Garrett, Adj.
H. Lee Parsons, Surg.
J. H. Bullock, Adj.
Joseph W. Mitchell, Chap., r. December 19, 1862
Andrew J. Whitthorne, A.S.
R. G. Norris, A.S., r. July 9, 1862
John A. Cheatham, Adj.
R. F. Richardson, A.S., dropped August 2, 1862
William I. [illegible], A.S.
Elisha Mayfield, A.Q.M., dropped June 10, 1864
Alex L. Hamilton, A.S.
Harnet Pinson, A.S.

Officers of Company A

James C. Thompson, Capt.
George D. Hardy, 1st Lt., r. July 29, 1862
John E. Price, 2nd Lt., Acting A.S.
Thomas J. Julian 2nd Lt.
Alphonzo C. Thompson, 2nd Lt., dropped June 23, 1862, r. August 2, 1862

Officers of Company B

Isaac N. McClendon, Capt., died May 8, 1862
R. G. Pattillo, Capt., Acting Adj., r. July 31, 1862
R. B. Thrasher, Capt.
Stephen Winstead, 2nd Lt.
William C. Lee, 2nd Lt.

Officers of Company C

M. C. Peel, Capt.
T. R. Lawrence, 1st Lt., deserted December 21, 1862
Henry F. Dickson, 2nd Lt., r March 25, 1863
G. M. Anderson, 2nd Lt.
W. T. Black, 1st Lt., r. May 18, 1862

Officers of Company D

Reed Fletcher, Capt., from 2nd Lt., Ninth Arkansas, r.
Joseph W. Wright, 1st Lt.
William P. Stephens, 2nd Lt.
William F. West, 2nd Lt., r. December 4, 1862
John R. Holland, 1st Lt., r. August 2, 1862
William G. Butler, 2nd Lt., r. August 4, 1862
John W. Hawley, 2nd Lt., Acting A. Q. M.

Officers of Company E

Felix R. Robertson, Capt.
Simon Rice, Capt., killed October 4, 1862
Charles I. Miller, Capt.
James C. Whaling, 2nd Lt.
James J. Gillcoat, 2nd Lt., r. May 26, 1862

Officers of Company F

John W. Barnett, Capt., r. December 31, 1862
John L. Brent, Capt.
W. H. Davidson, 2nd Lt., r. August 2, 1862
James A. Ashford, 2nd Lt.
James T. Taliaferro, 1st Lt.

Officers of Company G

Charles Lynch, Capt., died October 4, 1862
J. A. Baker, 1st Lt.
James W. Moore, Capt.
W. J. Turner, 1st Lt.

Officers of Company H

William N. Parish, Capt., to Lt. Col.
John B. Walker, Capt.
George W. Isaacs, 2nd Lt., killed
John W. Jay, 2nd Lt., r. September 26, 1862
Robert S. Farrar, 1st Lt.

Officers of Company I

Samuel H. Southerland, Capt., to Maj.
Lee Morgan, 1st Lt., r. December 26, 1862
R. B. Smith, 2nd Lt.
James E. Webb, 2nd Lt.

Officers of Company K

D. W. Carroll, Capt., to Col., April 2, 1862
W. F. Owen, Capt.
Lindsay H. Oliver, 1st Lt., to Maj., to Q.M.
George P. Atkins, 2nd Lt., r.
B. F. Hancock, 2nd Lt., r. August 22, 1862
James W. Hellums, 1st Lt.
T. H. Collier, 2nd Lt.

Note: Some of this company was transferred to Twelfth Battalion, Arkansas Sharpshooters in June 1862

NOTES

Chapter 1: Follow the Sun

Note 1, O. R. Volume XLIX/1, Pages 352-353

Note 2, O.R. Volume XLIX/1, Page 421

Note 3, O.R. Volume XLIX/1, Page 909

Note 4, Alabama Gen Web, Tuscaloosa County Home Page, Burning of the Campus in 1865

Note 5, 1860 Census Saline County, Saline Township, Page 136

Note 6, 1850 Census Mississippi, Marshall County, Southern Division, Page 263

Note 7, Mississippi Gen Web, Itawamba County Home Page

Note 8, Our Timberland Home by Elwin L. Goolsby, Page 108

Note 9, The Quitman Manuscript, Grant County Museum

Note 10, 1850 Census Mississippi, Marshall County, Southern Division, Page 263

Note 11, Early Settlers of Pickens County, Alabama, by James Delphos Johnson Jr.,

The Johnson book contains the first record of the Silas Isaacs family found in Alabama. The book lists records found in Pickens County, State of Alabama. Silas Isaacs purchased two parcels of land containing 40 acres each in Pickens County on February 2, 1836, and December 30, 1836. One of the parcels of land was located south of Pickens, Alabama. The description reads T19, R14, S34 and was purchased on December 30. The other parcel of land was located south of Carrollton, Alabama. The land description reads T21, R15, and S2 and was purchased on February 2.

Chapter 2: A Call to Arms

Note 1, The Autobiography of Sir Henry Morgan Stanley, edited by his wife, Dorothy Stanley, Pages 164-165

Note 2, Confederate Military Histories, Volume 10, Chapter 1

Note 3, Muster rolls of First Arkansas Mounted Rifles, Arkansas Historical Commission, Microfilm #317, Roll 9

Note 4, O. R. Volume III, No. 22, Report of Colonel T. J. Churchill, Page 110

Note 5, McRae's list of those who were hospitalized or absent, Arkansas Historical Commission

Note 6, Military records of 18th Arkansas' company muster rolls, Arkansas Historical Commission, Microfilm #317, Roll 158
Note 7, Marshall County, Mississippi, 1851, marriage records

Note 8, Saline County, Arkansas, marriage records book A-C 1836-1875

Note 9, 1860 Census Saline County, Saline Township, Page 136

Note 10, Confederate Veteran, Volume XVII, 1909, Reminiscence of an Arkansan, by R. T. Martin, member 18th Arkansas Infantry, Pages 69-70

Note 11, Letter by J. N. Parker 18th Arkansas, Archives Port Hudson State Commemorative Area

Note 12, Arkansas Gazette, April 12, 1862, Page 6, Column 1, Memphis and Little Rock Rail Road
"A regular tri-weekly line of First Class Steam Ships, will run between Memphis and DeValls Bluff, making this the most comfortable, expedition and cheapest route ever established between Memphis and Little Rock.
"Boats leave Memphis every Tuesday, Thursday and Saturday, at 5 o'clock p.m. passing DeValls Bluff en route to Des Arc and Jacksonport, every Monday, Thursday and Saturday.

"Returning boats pass DeValls Bluff every Monday, Wednesday and Saturday, making close connections with the cars at DeValls Bluff each way.

"Cars leave Little Rock everyday except Sunday, at 7:30 a.m. returning leave DeValls Bluff 2:30 o'clock p.m., arriving at Little Rock at 6:30 o'clock.

"Through tickets can be procured of J. L. Palmer, General Ticket Agent, "Anthony House," The Little Rock; and at the ticket office of the Memphis and Little Rock road 258 Main Street, Memphis.

"For freight apply to G. H. Meade, General Freight Agent, corner Markham and Scott Street. Anthony House block, Little Rock, and Larey Harmisted, steamship boat agent Memphis."

Note 13, The Arkansas Historical Quarterly, Volume VI, 1947, The Memphis and Little Rock Railroad During the Civil War, by Leo E. Huff

Note 14, Confederate Victories at Fort Pillow, Edited by Edward F. Williams

Note 15, Muster Rolls of the 18th Arkansas, Arkansas Historical Commission Microfilm #317, Roll 158

Note 16, Special Collection Division, University of Arkansas Libraries, Fayetteville, Arkansas, Arabella Lanktree Wilson Papers, 1823-1876, Compiled by Allen Scott

Note 17, Hempstead County Historical Society, Volume 12, E. F. Sanders Letter, 1988, Page 3

Note 18, Battles and Leaders of the Civil War, Volume 1, The Western Flotilla, by Henry Walke, Rear Admiral U. S. N., Page 449

Note 19, Confederate Victories at Fort Pillow, Edited by Edward F. Williams, Page 18

Note 20, Confederate Veteran, Volume VI, January 1898, Our Evacuation of Fort Pillow

Chapter 3: The Civil War Surgeon

Note 1, Saline County land and tax records 1858, List of persons and property assessed for taxes

Note 2, James L. Isaacs' letters, Arkansas History Commission

Note 3, Service records of Confederate generals and staff officers, Confederate States Army, Arkansas History Commission, Microfilm #M331, Roll 138

Note 4, The Roster of Confederate Soldiers 1861-1865, Volume 3, Page 342

Note 5, Descriptive list to be copied to the roster, Robert Lee Camp Records, Fort Worth Library

Note 6, Edward G. Gerdes Civil War Home Page http://www.couchgenweb. com/civilwar/

Note 7, Tennessee Historical Quarterly, Volume XLII, Military Hospitals in Memphis 1861-1865, By Patricia M. LaPointe, Page 326

Note 8, Confederate Victories at Fort Pillow, Edward F. Williams III

Notes 9 & 10, Tennessee Historical Quarterly, Volume XLII, Military Hospitals in Memphis 1861-1865, By Patricia M. LaPointe, Pages 329-330

Note 11, Confederate Veteran, Volume V, 1897, Page 522

Note 12, Tennessee Historical Quarterly, Volume XLII, Military Hospitals in Memphis 1861-1865, By Patricia M. LaPointe, Page 338

Note 13, The Photographic History of The Civil War, Volume IV, Field and Temporary Hospitals, by Deering J. Roberts, M.D. Surgeon, Confederate States Army, Pages 262-264

Note 14, Confederate Veteran, Volume XIII, 1905, Vivid War Experiences at Ripley, Page 263

Note 15, Service records of Confederate generals and staff officers, Confederate States Army, Arkansas History Commission, Microfilm #M331, Roll 138

Chapter 4: Retreat from Corinth and The Battle of Iuka

Note 1, Confederate Veteran, Volume XVII, 1909, Reminiscence of an Arkansan, by R. T. Martin, member 18th Arkansas Infantry, Pages 69-70

Note 2, O. R. Volume II, Record of Events, Page 601

Note 3, O. R. Volume XVII/I, No. 39, Report of Major General Sterling Price, Page 120

Note 4, Battles and Leaders of The Civil War, by Colonel Thomas L. Snead, Volume II, With Price East of the Mississippi, Page 724

Note 5, Battles and Leaders of The Civil War, by Colonel Thomas L. Snead, Volume II, With Price East of The Mississippi, Page 728

Note 6, O. R. Volume XVII/I, No. 39, Report of Major General Sterling Price, Page 120

Note 7, O. R. Volume XVII/I, No. 1, Report of Major General Ulysses S. Grant, Pages 65-66

Note 8, O. R. Volume XVII/I, No. 2, Report of Major General William S. Rosecrans, Page 73

Note 9, The Darkest Days of the War, Peter Cozzens, Page 87

Note 10, O. R. Volume XVII/I, No. 40, Report of Brigadier General Louis Hebert, Pages 124-125

Note 11, Battles and Leaders of The Civil War, by Colonel Thomas L. Snead, Volume II, With Price East of the Mississippi, Page 730

Note 12, Hempstead County Historical Society, Volume XI, Spring of 1987, Page 12

Note 13, O. R. Volume XVII/I, No. 2, Report of Major General William S. Rosecrans, Page 72

Note 14, O. R. Volume XVII/I, No. 52, Report of Brigadier General Dabney H. Maury, Pages 136-137

Note 15, The Darkest Days of the War, Peter Cozzens, Pages 133-134

Chapter 5: Fighting on Home Ground

Note 1, O. R. Volume II, Record of Events, Page 607

Note 2, 1850 Census of Marshall County, Mississippi, Page 263

Note 3, 1850 Census of Marshall County, Mississippi, Page 261B

Note 4, 1850 Census of Marshall County, Mississippi, Page 229

Note 5, 1850 Census of Marshall County, Mississippi, Page 263

Chapter 6: The Siege of Corinth

Notes 1 & 2, O. R. Volume XVII/1, No. 105, Report of Major General Earl
Van Dorn, Pages 377-378

Note 3, O. R. Volume XVII/1, No. 108, Report of Major General Sterling
Price, Pages 385-386

Note 4, O. R. Volume XVII/I, No. 2, Reports of Major General William S.
Rosecrans, Pages 166-167

Note 5, O. R. Volume XVII/I, No. 105, Reports of Major General Earl Van
Dorn, Pages 377-378

Note 6, O. R. Volume XVII/I, No. 105, Reports of Major General Earl Van
Dorn, Page 379

Note 7, Battles and Leaders of the Civil War, Volume II, The Battle Of
Corinth, by Major General William S. Rosecrans, Page 748

Note 8, O. R. Volume XVII/1, No. 108, Report of Major General Sterling
Price, Pages 386-387

Note 9, Battles and Leaders of the Civil War, Volume II, The Battle Of Corinth, by Major General William S. Rosecrans, Page 749

Chapter 7: Into the Mouth of the Cannon

Note 1, The Darkest Days of the War, by Peter Cozzens, Page 236

Note 2, The Darkest Days of the War, by Peter Cozzens, Page 241

Note 3, O. R. Volume XVII/1, No. 114, Report of Brigadier General William L. Cabell, Page 402

Note 4, O. R. Volume III, No. 22, Report of Colonel T. J. Churchill, Page 110

Note 5, Confederate Military History, Volume 10, Chapter 12, Page 351

Note 6, The Lost Account of the Battle of Corinth, Page 33

Note 7, Confederate Military History, Volume 10, Chapter 12, Page 352

Chapter 8: The Battle of Davis Bridge

Note 1, Brochure, Siege and Battle of Corinth Commission, A Guide to the Corinth Campaigns of 1862, by Stacy Allen

Note 2, The Darkest Days of the War, Peter Cozzens, Pages 278-280

Note 3, O. R. Volume XVII/1, No. 114, Report of Brigadier General William L. Cabell, Page 403

Note 4, Confederate Veteran, Volume XX, 1912, Page 121

Note 5, O. R. Volume XVII/1, No. 114 Report of Brigadier General William L. Cabell, Pages 403-404

Note 6, The Darkest Days of the War, Peter Cozzens, Page 292

Note 7, J. N. Parker Letter, Port Hudson State Commemorative Area Archives

Note 8, Port Hudson State Commemorative Area, Port Hudson Its History, Lieutenant Howard C. Wright, 1863, Page 59

Note 9, Confederate Veteran, Volume XIII, 1905, Page 262

Note 10, O. R. Volume XVII/1, Pages 404-405

Note 11, True Democrat, March 4, 1863, Arkansas History Commission, Little Rock

Chapter 9: Port Hudson: A Confederate Fortress on the Mississippi

Note 1, O.R. Volume XVII/2, Operations in West Tennessee and Northern Mississippi, Pages 734-735

Note 2, Confederate Veteran, Volume XVII, 1909, Reminiscence of an Arkansan, by R. T. Martin, 18th Arkansas Infantry, Pages 69-70

Note 3, Port Hudson Confederate Bastion on the Mississippi, by Lawrence Lee Hewitt, Page 15

Note 4, Port Hudson Confederate Bastion on the Mississippi, by Lawrence Lee Hewitt, Page 20

Note 5, O.R. Volume, XVII/I, No. 106, Return of Casualties, Page 383

Notes 6, 7, Confederate Military History, Volume 10, Chapter 10

Note 8, Muster Roles 18th Arkansas, Arkansas History Commission, Microfilm #317, Roll 158 P-Y

Note 9, Port Hudson Confederate Bastion on the Mississippi, by Lawrence Lee Hewitt, Page 41

Note 10, Confederate Military History, Volume 10, Chapter 9

Note 11, Port Hudson Confederate Bastion on the Mississippi, by Lawrence Lee Hewitt, Pages 41-42

Note 12, Confederate Veteran, Volume XVII, 1909, Page 69

Note 13, Confederate Veteran, Volume XXVII, 1919, Under Fire at Port Hudson, by J. M. M'Neilly, Page 337

Note 14, Confederate Veteran, Volume XXVII, 1919, Under Fire at Port Hudson, by J. M. M'Neilly, Page 337

Note 15, Fort Hudson Confederate Bastion on the Mississippi, by Lawrence Lee Hewitt, Page 49

Note 16, Dr. James L. Isaacs' letters, Arkansas History Commission

Note 17, Official Records of the Union and Confederate Navy in The War of Rebellion, Series 1, Volume 19, West Gulf Blockading Squadron, Pages 666-667

Note 18, O.R. Volume XV, Beall's Brigade, Pages 1032-33,

Note 19, Confederate Veteran, Volume XXVII, 1919, Under Fire at Port Hudson, By J. M. M'Neilly, Page 337

Note 20, Official Records of the Union and Confederate Navy in The War of Rebellion, Series 1, Volume 19, West Gulf Blockading Squadron, Pages 666-667

Note 21, Confederate Veteran, Volume VI, 1898, Ships That Passed at Night, Pages 250-251

Note 22, Port Hudson Campaign 1862-1863, Edward Cunningham, Page 26

Note 23, O.R. Volume XV, Report of Major General Nathaniel P. Banks, Page 252

Note 24, O.R. Volume XV, Report of Major General Franklin Garner, Page 277

Note 25, Port Hudson Campaign 1862-1863, Edward Cunningham, Page 26

Note 26, Confederate Veteran, Volume VI, 1898, Ships That Passed at Night, Pages 250-251

Note 27, Port Hudson Campaign 1862-1863, Edward Cunningham, Page 27

Note 28, Port Hudson Confederate Bastion on the Mississippi, Lawrence Lee Hewitt, Pages 76-81

Note 29, Confederate Veteran, Volume VII, 1919, Under Fire at Port Hudson, J. H. M'Neilly, Page 337

Note 30, O. R. Volume XV, Gardner's Reports, Pages 272-278

Note 31, Official Records of the Union and Confederate Navy, Series 1, Volume 19, Report of Captain Alden, Pages 672-673

Note 32, Official Records of the Union and Confederate Navy in The War of Rebellion, Series 1, Volume 19, West Gulf Blockading Squadron, Page 667

Note 33, Confederate Veteran, Volume XXVI, 1918, Hot Shot at Port Hudson, W. R. Campbell, Page 288

Note 34, Confederate Veteran, Volume XXVII, 1919, Under Fire at Port Hudson, J. H. M'Neilly, Page 337

Note 35, William N. Parish Letter, Arkansas History Commission, SMC Box V #16

Chapter 10: The Big Bushwhack

Note 1, Port Hudson State Commemorative Area, Port Hudson Its History, Lieutenant Howard C. Wright 1863, Page 25

Note 2, O. R. Volume XXVI/I, No 41, Col. O. P. Lyles, 23rd Arkansas Infantry, Page 151

Note 3, Port Hudson State Commemorative Area, Map of Port Hudson Port 1864

Note 4, Port Hudson State Commemorative Area, Port Hudson Its History, Lieutenant Howard C. Wright 1863, Pages 25-26

Note 5, Port Hudson Confederate Bastion on the Mississippi, by Lawrence Lee Hewitt, Page 138

Note 6, Port Hudson State Commemorative Area, Port Hudson Its History, by Lieutenant Howard C. Wright, 1863, Page 32

Note 7, O. R. Volume XXVI/I, No. 1, Major General P. Banks, Page 43

Note 8, Port Hudson Confederate Bastion on the Mississippi, by Lawrence Lee Hewitt, Page 141

Note 9, The Darkest Days of the War, by Peter Cozzens, Page 319

Note 10, Battles and Leaders of the Civil War, Volume III, Pages 593-594

Note 11, Port Hudson Campaign, by Edward Cunningham, Page 57

Note 12, Port Hudson State Commemorative Area, Port Hudson Its History, Lieutenant Howard C. Wright, 1863, Page 33

Note 13, Port Hudson State Commemorative Area, Port Hudson Its History, Lieutenant Howard C. Wright, 1863, Pages 32-34

Note 14, Confederate Veteran, Volume V, 1897, The Siege of Port Hudson, Page 174

Chapter 11: Trying to Hold Their Ground

Note 1, O. R. Volume XXVI/1, No 41, Report of Colonel I. G. W. Steedman, Page 158

Note 2, Confederate Veteran, Volume XVII, 1909, Reminiscence of an Arkansan, Page 70

Note 3, Foxes Regimental Losses

Note 4, Confederate Veteran, Volume XVII, 1909, Reminiscence of an Arkansan, Page 70

Note 5, O. R. Volume XXVI/1, No. 41, Report of Colonel I. G. W. Steedman, Page 161

Note 6, Confederate Veteran, Volume XVII, 1909, Reminiscence of an Arkansan, Page 69

Note 7, Confederate Veteran, Volume XVII, 1909, Port Hudson Calamities-Mule Meat, Page 512

Note 8, Recollections of Ozan, by Newton Wallace, Reynolds Family Archives

Note 9, O. R. Volume XXVI/1, No. 40, Pages 154-155

Note 10, Confederate Veteran, Volume VIII, 1900, Page 230

Note 11, O. R. Volume XXVI/1, No. 35, Lewis J. Girard, Pages 145-146

Chapter 12: Trouble on the Line

Note 1, J. N. Parker Letter, Port Hudson State Commemorative Area Archives

Note 2, O. R. Volume XXVI/1, No. 41, Reports of Colonel I. G. W. Steedman, Pages 158-159

Note 3, O. R. Volume XXVI/1, No. 41, Reports of Colonel I. G. W. Steedman, Page 161

Note 4, O. R. Volume XXVI/1, No. 41, Reports of Colonel I. G. W. Steedman,
Page 162

Note 5, Arkansas Historical Quarterly, Volume 4, 1945, Arkansas Defends the Mississippi, by Fred Harvey Herrington, Page 114

Note 6, Arkansas Historical Quarterly, Volume 4, 1945, Arkansas Defends the Mississippi, by Fred Harvey Herrington, Page 115

Note 7, Arkansas Historical Quarterly, Volume 4, 1945, Arkansas Defends the Mississippi, by Fred Harvey Herrington, Page 115

Note 8, O. R. Volume XXVI/1, No. 46, Reports of Colonel W. R. Miles, Pages 176-177

Note 9, Confederate Veteran, Volume V, 1897, The Siege of Port Hudson, Colonel E. C. McDowell, Page 174

Note 10, O. R. Volume XXVI/1, No. 36, Reports of General W. N. Beall, Pages 146-147

Note 11, O. R. Volume XXVI/1, No. 41, Reports of Colonel I. G. W. Steedman
Pages 163-164

Note 12, Confederate Military History, Volume 10, Chapter 12, Page 335

Note 13, O. R. Volume XXVI/1, No. 36, Reports of General W. N. Beall, Page 148

Note 14, Battles and Leaders of the Civil War, Volume III, The Capture of Port Hudson, by Lieutenant Colonel Richard R. Irwin U. S. V., Page 597

Chapter 13: Trip Back Home

Note 1, The Port Hudson Campaign, by Edward Cunningham, Page 121

Note 2, Muster Rolls 18th Arkansas, Arkansas History Commission, Microfilm #317, Roll 158 P-Y

Note 3, Philippians 3:13b-14, KJV

Note 4, Arkansas Methodist, May 29, 1897, Page 15, Column 2, Arkansas History Commission, Little Rock

Chapter 14: The Hardships of Southern Women

Note 1, The Photographic History of the Civil War, The Military Telegraph, by Major General A. W. Greely U.S.A., Page 348

Note 2, O. R. Volume XV, Series 1, General Order 2, Pages 780-781

Note 3, Battles and Leaders of the Civil War, Volume II, The Opening of the Lower Mississippi, by Admiral David D. Porter, Pages 22-23

Note 4, Confederate Women in Arkansas in the Civil War 1907, How Women Supported the Family, Microfilm #D1R2, Garland County Library

Note 5, Confederate Women in Arkansas in the Civil War 1907, Microfilm #D1R2, Garland County Library

Note 6, Confederate Cavalry West of the River, by Stephen Oates

Note 7, Clark County Historical Journal - 1994, The Ragged Colonel of the Rawhides

Note 8, Muster Rolls 18th Arkansas, Microfilm #317, Roll 158, Arkansas History Commission

Note 9, Arkansas Methodist, April 26, 1894, Page 3, Column 2, Microfilm Arkansas History Commission

Note 10, Oath of Allegiance to Federal Government, Richard T. Stockton's Military Record, Microfilm #317, Roll 158, Arkansas Historical Commission

Note 11, Arkansas 1870 Census, Grant County, Calvert Township

Note 12, The Civil War in Arkansas, Web Site

Note 13, Confederate Women in Arkansas in the Civil War 1907, Microfilm #D1R2, Garland County Library

Note 14, Arkansas Historical Quarterly, Volume 7, 1948, Early Days in Grant County

Epilogue

Jenkins Ferry: The Final Battles in Saline County

Note 1, O. R. Volume XXXIV/1, All Reports Series #61, No. 2, Report of Major General Nathaniel P. Banks, Pages 178-180

Note 2, O. R. Volume XXXIV/1, No. 93, Report of Brigadier General E. Kirby Smith, Pages 476-477

Note 3, O. R. Volume XXXIV/1, No. 48, Report of Major General Sterling Price, Pages 779-782

Note 4, O. R. Volume XXXIV/1, No. 20, Report of Lieutenant Colonel Adolph Dengler, Forty-third Illinois Infantry, Page 736

Note 5, O. R. Volume XXXIV/1, No. 34, Report of Colonel Samuel J. Crawford, Second Kansas Colored Infantry, Pages 757-759

Note 6, Arkansas Historical Quarterly, Volume 7, 1948, Early Days in Grant County

Note 7, Our Timberland Home, by Elwin L. Goolsby, Page 64

Note 8, The Civil War Day by Day, by E. B. Long, With Barbara Long

Note 9, Clark County Historical Journal, 1994, The Ragged Colonel of the Rawhides

Note 10, Arkansas Gazette, Sunday, November 1938, by Winnie Sparks

BIBLIOGRAPHY

Material researched by the author

Christ, Mark K., Rugged and Sublime-The Civil War in Arkansas, University of Arkansas Press, 1994

Cozzens, Peter, The Darkest Days of the War, The University of North Carolina Press, North Carolina, 1997

Confederate Military History, Guild Press, Carmel, Indiana, 1997

Confederate Women in Arkansas in The Civil War 1861-1865, The United Confederate Veterans of Arkansas, November, 1907

Cunningham, Edward, Port Hudson Campaign 1862-1863, Louisiana State University Press, Baton Rouge, Louisiana, 1987

Foxes Regimental Losses, Guild Press, Carmel, Indiana, 1997

Goolsby Elwin L., Our Timberland Home, A History of Grant County, Rose Publishing Company, Little Rock, Arkansas

Hewitt, Lawrence Lee, Port Hudson Confederate Bastion on the Mississippi, Louisiana State University Press, Baton Rouge, Louisiana, 1994

Hurst, Jack, Nathan Bedford Forrest A Biography, Vintage Books, New York, 1993

Johnson, James Delphos, Early Settlers of Pickens County, Alabama

LaPointe, Patricia M., From Saddlebags To Science: A Century Of Health Care In Memphis, 1830-1930, The Health Sciences Museum Foundation, Memphis, Tennessee, 1984

McPherson, James M., What They Fought For 1861-1865, Anchor Books Doubleday, New York, 1995

Oats, Stephen B., Confederate Cavalry West of the River, University of Texas Press, 1961

Stanley, Henry Morgan, The Autobiography of Sir Henry Morgan Stanley, edited by his wife, Dorothy Stanley, Houghton Mifflin Company, New York

Steele, Phillip W., The Civil War in Arkansas, Pelican Publishing Company, Gretna, Louisiana, 1993

Sifakis, Stewart, Compendium of the Confederate Armies: Florida and Arkansas, Facts on File, New York, 1992

The Photographic History of the Civil War, The Military Telegraph, Prisons and Hospitals, Volume IV, The Blue And Gray Press, Secaucus, New Jersey, 1887

The Roster of Confederate Soldiers 1861-1865

Williams, Edward F., Confederate Victories at Fort Pillow, Nathan Bedford Forrest Hiking Trails, Inc., Memphis, Tennessee, 1894

Willis, James, Arkansas Confederates in the Western Theater, Morningside, 1998

Wright, Howard C., Port Hudson Its History 1863, Port Hudson State Commemorative Area, Louisiana, reprint, 1978

Index

ABOUT THE AUTHOR

The author has a lifelong interest in Civil War History and is the publisher and editor of Reynolds Archives, an Internet site. He has written historical articles about early American History that is published on his home pages. Also included on his site, are short biographies and essays about his family. He is a member of the Garland County Historical Society. He is the associate editor for Travel Host Magazine of Hot Springs, Arkansas and has written for the magazine and local newspapers.

http://www.reynoldsarchive.com

Printed in the United States
66140LVS00005B/232-255

9 781425 906054